# The World of Wizards

# THE WORLD OF WIZARDS

## Modern magical tools and ancient traditions

ANTON AND MINA ADAMS

MetroBooks

# Contents

# introduction –
# what are wizards and
# what do they do?

Sometimes respected, sometimes feared, Wizards have had a varied reputation over the centuries. Seen as wise or superstitious, benevolent or cruel, they have long fascinated the world.

The term "Wizard" — although not in common use in the magic community since the nineteenth century — refers to the men who have practiced and studied the occult, or magic. Wizards can equally be referred to as magicians, sorcerers or Witches. While the term "Wizard" itself is used exclusively to describe men, the wisdom they have attained is information that can be — and has been — used by both Witches and Wizards, and is not gender specific.

Often what is considered magical in one century may become commonplace in the next century. The scientists of today may well have been regarded as Wizards in centuries past. In essence, the best Wizards have been those who have had keen minds, and have been able to free their thoughts from everyday struggles and ponder on the bigger issues of life. This ability was prized in the old world of villages and other small communities, as it was recognized as making the community better able to survive various calamities and ills.

The Wizard's power has come first of all from observation. Much magical lore is built on the fundamental belief that, if we can understand the flow of the energies of the earth and how these energies work in harmony, we can gain enormous insight and power. Observing, among other things, the patterns of the weather, the migration patterns of birds and the behavior of people around him, has gained the Wizard — in the eyes of those focused only on the reality of day-to-day survival — the uncanny "magical" ability of being able to see into the future. In fact, the Wizard has often been doing little more than paying very close attention to the present.

Wizards have also impressed with their intense belief in several levels of reality — that of the ordinary world, the extraordinary world of fairies, elves and other spirit entities, the hierarchy of the angels, and the realm of the higher being. Many Wizards have attempted to rise above earthly concerns and focus on the spiritual world, forging links between the world of the living and that of the dead. Angels and the fairy folk are also believed to be the allies of various Wizards. Communication with beings from other dimensions has been taken seriously, and studied in depth.

How he chose to use his education, experience and power was up to the individual Wizard. At one end of the spectrum, he could tap into, and manipulate, a strong form of psychic energy in order to discover the meaning of life. At the other, he might do little more than make a living by amusing and flattering clients with glimpses into their future. If he was wise and had integrity and compassion in his dealings with others, the Wizard would be revered.

There have been a number of Wizards who chose to use their power less than ethically. As most did not survive their experiences, one of the most important magical maxims evolved: whatever a Wizard sends out returns to him three times over.

This book focuses on the wisdom of the Wizards through the ages. We shall examine those Wizards, both mythical and real, and important scholars who have made major contributions to our understanding of the psychic energy of the earth and the Cosmos. We shall also look at the practical approaches, used for centuries by wise Wizards, to harnessing psychic energy in order to enrich the physical and spiritual well-being of those who seek their wisdom.

# Chapter I
# Famous Wizards: Past & Present

## Introduction: A Wizard's Life

As in many other professions, there are wise Wizards and those who are not so astute. Also, as in many other walks of life, those Wizards who attracted most attention were the few who walked a less than honorable path.

There are innumerable accounts of Wizards, such as Faust, their minds turned toward malicious and harmful practices, who would consort with malevolent spirits, make pacts with the Devil, cast an "evil eye" upon unyielding maidens, and generally practice the darker aspects of magic. These darker aspects fundamentally involve casting spells, making amulets and talismans, and uttering incantations, all to the end of gaining power to manipulate others for the Wizard's own ends. However, time and time again stories of such Wizards conclude with the magician coming to a rather sticky, mysterious end.

These tales are not just morality stories devised to teach us what happens when we are bad. They should also be treated as testimonies to the fact that the wizard's manipulation of or the interference in another person's life, will or purpose may destroy or, at the very least, lead him to his being considered a charlatan or a fool.

Wise Wizards, however, practice magic to enhance a person's or group's true purpose or "will." A compassionate Wizard, like Merlin, is able to divine true purposes, and will use spells, incantations, amulets and talismans to support that purpose. The "true purpose" is a complex concept; in brief, it is the purpose for which a person or a group is in this world — a beneficial purpose.

Some Wizards through the ages have had to suffer a certain amount of enmity, dread and derision — the Count of Saint-Germaine is one — but others, such as King Solomon and Vergil, have been regarded with respect and awe.

Some have studied the magic of herbs and the energies of the earth, while others have explored the movement of the stars and the angels. These studies of what were considered to be hidden mysteries attracted not only Wizards, but scholars as well. Agrippa von Nettesheim, Theophrastus Paracelsus, and Robert Fludd all wrote key mystical texts, though they did not practice the magical arts.

However, some Wizards, such as Eliphas Lévi, Aleister Crowley, and Gerald Gardner combined both areas of endeavor. They were practitioners of magic as well as authors of seminal works that helped revive interest in the "hidden mysteries." Alex Sanders brought a certain flamboyance to such studies and Oberon Zell Ravenheart established an influential magazine that sought to increase understanding of and reverence for the power of nature.

# SOLOMON

The name "King Solomon" has been one of the most influential in the Wizard's world. It is the name lent to a very important magical "seal" or talisman, a hexagram symbolizing the balance of magical forces, which has been used as a protective talisman for centuries. It is also the name attached to a very important grimoire (book of spells and magical techniques) called *The Key of Solomon The King* (see page 86).

King Solomon was a King of Israel who ruled in Jerusalem in the tenth century BC. A real person in history, he had a great number of superhuman qualities attributed to him.

The son of David and Bathsheba, Solomon steered Israel into one of its Golden Ages by making astute political alliances through a number of marriages. He had excellent organizational abilities in government and the army, and a healthy dose of showmanship.

Tapping into the riches of his land and those of his neighbors, Solomon embarked on a vast building program in Jerusalem that culminated in the building of the famous Temple of Solomon in c 950 BC. This Temple, with ceilings, walls, and floors covered with gold, was believed to house the name of God and was dedicated to the God of the Israelites. It was also

### THE WISDOM OF SOLOMON

*There are many stories about Solomon's wisdom. When asked to decide which of two women was the mother of a child, Solomon reached for his sword to cut the infant in half so each woman could have her share. By observing the facial expressions of both women, Solomon was able to divine which one was the real mother.*

believed to house the Ark of the Covenant (a casket holding, according to the Bible, the Ten Commandments).

Solomon was charming, witty, and a quick thinker, and had a great lust for wisdom. Considered a man wiser than all others, he was allegedly given great wisdom by the teachings of an angel, who was also responsible for giving him a magical ring that lent him the power to control various spirits. It was apparently this power that allowed Solomon to unleash spirits to help with the building of the Temple.

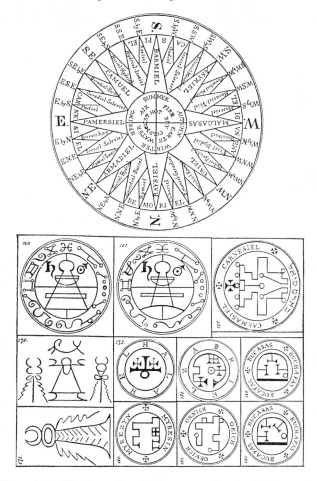

The symbols of The Lesser Key of Solomon are referred to in white magic.

# MERLIN

B ritain of long ago was a country torn in battle. The longing for a wise prophet able to right its wrongs led the figure of Merlin, an archetypal trickster and magician, to occupy a powerful position in British myths. Possibly a real-life oracle living during the second half of the sixth century AD, Merlin is known as the world's best-known magician.

His origins, like his actual existence, are uncertain but he has a central role in literary works that link him with the equally legendary Camelot, King Arthur, Excalibur, the Holy Grail and the Knights of the Round Table.

In the 1130s, Geoffrey of Monmouth wrote a history of the Kings of Britain, outlining the exploits and prophecies of Merlin, a supposedly fatherless boy who was able to prophesy the futures of kings. He is said to have lifted the stones of Ireland with his strong magical powers and transported them to the site upon which Stonehenge was constructed.

This explanation for how Stonehenge was built has long been dismissed as fanciful. However, Merlin's role as guardian of the true heirs to the British throne has continued to hold the imagination.

In Geoffrey of Monmouth's history, Merlin played an important role in British history during a particularly turbulent time when the country was torn between the followers of Vortigern and the rightful heirs, two boys known as Aurelius Ambrosius and Uther Pendragon. To manage the civic unrest Vortigern employed Saxon mercenaries, who eventually took control of the land.

In an attempt to strengthen his lair, Vortigern built a tower. However, the tower was unstable and, following the advice of his court magicians, Vortigen sought a boy with no father so that his blood could be sprinkled on the stones to stop the tower from falling down.

The fatherless boy eventually found in the south of Wales was Merlin, who instead saved Vortigern's life by divining that the tower's unsteadiness was due to a pool of water at its base. He further predicted that Vortigern would lose his life. Aurelius Ambrosius and Uther Pendragon eventually killed Vortigern, and the two rightful heirs returned to the throne.

Soon after, Merlin became instrumental in arranging the events that would lead to the birth of Arthur, the King under whom Britain would know its finest hour. When Arthur was born, Merlin became his guardian and an important guide for the future King.

According to legend, Merlin was the one who found Excalibur and was responsible for the construction of the Round Table. Merlin never died, but he disappeared, and is believed to have taken with him for safekeeping the Thirteen Treasures of Britain, including the Mantle of Arthur, which made the wearer invisible.

In other legends, it is believed that Merlin succumbed to the charms of an enchantress, who trapped him in a crystal cave or oak tree. It is believed that he is resting until he is again called to come to Britain's aid.

Merlin reveals the sectets of his magic to Vivien, who promptly deserts him.

# VERGIL

Publius Vergilius Maro, or Vergil, is best known as the author of one of the most highly revered and longest poems, the *Aeneid*, which was almost completed by his early death in 19 BC at 49 years. The poem traces the tribulations of Aeneas, and his mythical founding of the Roman state. Vergil is known for his studies in law, medicine, mathematics and philosophy, and for other works, including the *Eclogues*, which were written in 39 BC. This text in particular impressed the Catholic Church with Vergil's so-called power of prophecy, as it was believed to foretell the birth of Christ.

In Dante's *Commedia,* or "Divine Comedy," the character of Vergil appears as Dante's guide and master through Hell and Purgatory. Vergil's connection with Hell is strengthened by other stories of his magical abilities. It was said that he learnt magic from twelve devils, whom he released from a bottle found on his estate. He was further believed to have studied magic with a famous sorcerer who lived on the Mountain of Sorrows.

Vergil was also believed to be a very competent alchemist and metallurgist, with the power to breathe life into inanimate objects that he had constructed to do his bidding. Iron or copper horses were given the ability to trample thieves and metal statues were granted the power to guard his treasure. He was reputed to have a huge fortune; this may have come about because he had a number of important patrons, including Emperor Augustus, attracted by his fame.

As with many Wizards before and after him, Vergil became adept at using magic to help him escape censure and lynch mobs. Some of his famous escapes seemed miraculous. They included his ability to magically stop vengeful pursuers on the spot, to disappear into a bucket of water, or to escape prison by sailing away in a boat he drew on the wall of his cell.

Born and reared near Mantua, Vergil moved away from his home to study in Rome and finally settled in Naples, where he

Vergil shows Dante the condemned suffering in the inferno.

wrote the *Aeneid* in his final decade. The text of the epic poem contained a number of references to magic, including the combination of powerful herbs and the magic arts to change a person's form, and the use of a magic wand for drawing ghosts from hollow graves.

Vergil himself was credited with many magical marvels in Naples, from making a talisman in the shape of a golden leech to protect the city from a leech plague to founding a school for Wizards. He was also credited with founding the city, and building the Castell del'Oro – literally translated, the Egg Castle. This imposing fortress was popularly believed to have been built by Vergil, who was said to have balanced the whole structure on an egg. Vergil was buried in Naples, and his tomb has been the focus of religious pilgrimages.

# FAUST

Mephistopheles, the Devil by any other name, lures Faust into bargaining his soul.

tories of an archetypal all-powerful and all-knowing Wizard
have been with us since ancient times. Each generation has
been fascinated by the reputed magical exploits of Wizards
such as Merlin and Faust.

There are many stories and legends about Faust. Some believe
that he is a fictional character, first made popular in 1587 in a
book by Johann Spies called *Historia von D. Johann Fausten*,
published in Frankfurt. Others believe that the stories were
actually based on a real person, or a combination of people who
lived in the first half of the sixteenth century.

The central character is known in many countries by a number
of different but related names, such as Dr Faust, Dr Faustus,

and Dr Johann Fausten. A common theme in the myth, irrespective of the name and the minor details of the story, is the acquisition of knowledge by making a pact with the Devil.

The story of Dr Faust is a powerful mix of old myths and legends. It has the same theme as the biblical story of Adam and Eve, in which the couple eat from the Tree of Knowledge, doing so against God's express wishes but with the encouragement of Devil, who appears in the form of a snake. A number of Faust's reputed powers are the same as those attributed to Wizards such as Merlin (see pages 12–13), Vergil (see pages 14–15) and Henry Cornelius Agrippa von Nettesheim (see pages 18–19).

Johann Spies's book describes the rise and fall of Dr Fausten, a learned scholar of medicine, mathematics, astrology, sorcery, and prophecy. His already vast grasp of available knowledge merely leaves him thirsting for more. One night between nine and ten, at a crossroads near a dark forest, Dr Fausten conjures up the Devil by drawing a series of circles with his staff. When the Devil confronts him, Dr Fausten has the presence of mind to make a pact with him.

He asks the Devil to serve him for the term of his life and to provide him with the information he desires. In return, the Devil sets his own terms of the bargain — that the Doctor will only live for twenty-four years more, and that he must renounce the Christian faith. The doctor seals the pact by signing the document in his own blood.

From that moment, Dr Fausten lives a charmed life, acquiring comfort, luxury, fame, and fortune. He becomes known for his uncanny accuracy as an astrologer and as a traveler to distant stars. However, he also indulges in excess and decadence, and dies twenty-four years after the night on which the pact was signed. The story has a moral. Dr Fausten pays the price for his luxurious life and acquired knowledge. He dies a horrible death, and is found by his students in a gory mess, with his soul damned for eternity.

# AGRIPPA

**H**enry Cornelius Agrippa von Nettesheim is best known as the author of an important work on the occult called *De Occulta Philosophia* ("Occult Philosophy"). Written in 1510, when Agrippa was twenty-four years of age, the manuscript encapsulated magical thinking up to the beginning of the Renaissance period, and had a profound effect on Western occultism. It was eventually published circa 1530, just before the author's death.

Agrippa's *De Occulta* challenged the concepts behind the infamous *Malleus Maleficarum*, published twenty-four years earlier. This book, *The Hammer of the Witches*, was a poisonous text used by inquisitors to identify and destroy what were perceived to be Witchcraft practices in the late fifteenth and early sixteenth centuries. The central premise of this destruction was the idea that the practice of magic was synonymous with the worship of the Devil, and should be eradicated in the name of God.

In *De Occulta Philosophia*, Agrippa outlined his belief that magic had nothing to do with the Devil, but relied on will power, imagination, and the study of nature. He wrote many treatises and books, and these often earned him the censure of the Catholic Church and its monks. Born in Cologne in 1486, he led an unsettled life owing to his "heretical" views. He traveled to Italy, France, Switzerland, and England during his lifetime and took up posts in a number of leading European cities, such as Geneva, Antwerp, and Metz.

In Metz, Agrippa was instrumental in proving the innocence of a woman who had been accused of witchcraft simply because she was the daughter of a Witch. Her accusers were fined a paltry sum, and Agrippa left Metz in disgust with the inquisitors, referring to them as enemies of learning and true merit.

Agrippa, like many Wizards before and after him, was a scholar who thrived on acquiring knowledge in many fields,

such as astrology (see pages 104–106), numerology (see pages 116–117), and the Kabbalah (see pages 118–119). He also studied law and physics, and was believed to have obtained knowledge in almost all arts and sciences, including alchemy (see pages 92–93).

He was also fascinated by the search for the Philosopher's Stone (see pages 96–97), a magical and powerful substance that had many wonderful properties, including the ability to transform base metal into gold and to heal any disease.

As with many Wizards, both historical and mythical, Agrippa was also believed to have magical powers, such as the ability to pay his way during his travels with small bits of horn that gave the illusion of real money. He was also believed to have practiced necromancy, the art of contacting or reanimating the dead. This eventually led to the view that he was a black magician and, in one instance, to his being suspected of murder (see page 85).

Henrich Cornelius Agrippa, alchemist, doctor, kabbalist and Rosicrucian. Portrait from the title page of his *De Occulta Philosophia*, circa 1530.

# PARACELSUS

Paracelsus, born Phillipus Aureolus Theophrastus Bombastus von Hohenheim, was an early sixteenth century scholar and doctor. His view of the spiritual and physical connection between humans and the Cosmos was an important step in the development of knowledge about the practice of magic.

However, ego got in the way of his achieving harmony with his fellow scholars and surgeons, and von Hohenheim apparently devised the name Paracelsus to indicate that he was beyond the skill of the celebrated ancient Roman physician called Celsus. He may well have been, as his theories about healing the body and the soul to attain health were more akin to modern conceptions of health than to those of his contemporaries.

Born in Switzerland in a village near Zurich, Paracelsus first studied with an abbot celebrated for his writings on the Kabbalah (see pages 118–119). Although not an active Wizard, Paracelsus went on to study the same fields that interested Wizards, such as medicine, surgery, and chemistry. According to one source, his interest in metals led him to undertake a major journey to a huge number of mines in countries such as Germany and Hungary, in order to learn about the qualities and properties of the metals mined. Another source indicates that the mines employed him as an analyst.

His interest in alchemy led him to develop the use of minerals such as mercury in his search for potions to heal his patients. Mercury was successful in treating such conditions as syphilis. He was also fascinated by the concept of the Philosopher's Stone, or "Azoth" (see pages 96–97), a magical substance, and the Catholicon, a magical elixir, which were both reputed to be able to heal any illness. The Philosopher's Stone is also believed to give immortal life. It was believed that Paracelsus succeeded in his search for the Philosopher's Stone when he learned its secret from an Arabian Wizard in Constantinople.

Engraved portrait of Phillipus Aureolus Theophrastus Bombastus von Hohenheim, better known as Paracelsus (1493–1541). He was a leading herbalist, occultist and alchemist.

Paracelsus's medical discoveries and theories were finally published in 1536, in a book called *Die grosse Wundartzney*, where he linked the state of good health with the achievment of harmony with nature. Having studied astrology, he also believed that the Cosmos, and particularly the patterns and movements of the stars and planets, had a profound effect on life and matter.

His main contribution to occult thinking was his belief in and study of "natural magic." He believed that this form of "magic" came from God and that doctors could direct its power to the patient if they could tap into this energy.

Paracelsus officially died in 1541, under mysterious circumstances. Some believe that he was murdered, either through poison or by a fatal push. However, Francis Barrett, in his seminal work *The Magus*, published in 1801 with the subtitle *A Complete System of Occult Philosophy* (see pages 84–85), quaintly noted that Paracelsus, though entombed, still lives a quiet life, hidden away from the vices and follies of humankind.

# DR JOHN DEE

D
r John Dee was better known as a learned scholar and a celebrated astrologer at the court of Queen Elizabeth I than as a Wizard. However, his association with Edward Kelly, a medium and possibly a charlatan, led him into the realms of Wizardry.

In particular, Dr Dee studied how to acquire the ability to contact certain spirits or angels so that he could gain knowledge of how to transform metals into gold by the use of the Philosopher's Stone. Always short of money, he also sought to contact the angels so they could help him find buried treasure.

Dr Dee's knowledge of astrology, mathematics, alchemy, and his growing library devoted to the occult also led him to be accused of enchantment, charlatanism, and consorting with demons. He was imprisoned for the attempted murder of Queen Mary by sorcery, and accused of murdering small children with malevolent spells, but was acquitted.

Avowing no real psychic abilities himself, Dr Dee joined forces with Edward Kelly and a number of other mediums so that he could contact the spirits or angels. Being a devout Christian, Dr Dee was not interested in contacting demons, only benevolent entities who could help him find a means of unlimited financial support, such as the Philosopher's Stone.

With Kelly, Dr Dee embarked on a journey to the ruins of Glastonbury. They found what they believed to be the Philosopher's Stone, which they identified as powder contained in a vial. By using just a miniscule amount of the "powder of projection," they were said to be able to transform an ounce and a quarter of mercury into pure gold. However, although they possessed the powder used to transform the mercury, they did not know how to make more.

They continued their experiments, with Dr Dee recording their conduct and Kelly summoning the spirits by scrying (a

form of divination) in a crystal mirror. Messages were apparently spelled backwards when received. It was claimed it was important that the messages were so spelled, to mask the fact that special angelic knowledge was being communicated to humans.

After some time, Dr Dee and Kelly divined that there was a hierarchy of planes of angelic existence, each plane guarded by a particular group of angels, varying in power according to how high up in the hierarchy they were. The hierarchy was complex, and required special incantations and sigils (magical symbols) before a human could have access to the angels and their knowledge.

Together they evolved a complex angelic language which was first called "Angelic" (the language known in the Garden of Eden), and then came to be known as "Enochian," named after the biblical visionary called Enoch. The two Books of Enoch were Old Testament texts that were no longer accepted as part of the Bible, the second book in particular describing Enoch's travel through the seven tiers of heaven. A system of Enochian magic was developed where Wizards worked through the 30 planes of angelic existence, gathering magical knowledge.

The title page of Dr John Dee's famous collection of theorems on the Monas, which was supposed to incorporate all esoteric lore in the one sigil. From the *Monas Hieroglyphica*, 1564.

# ROBERT FLUDD

**R**obert Fludd was a great scholar, physician, alchemist, and astrologer who lived in England during the time of Elizabeth I. He was greatly interested in the Kabbalah (see pages 118–119), the theories of Paracelsus (see pages 20–21), and the tenets of Hermetic philosophy.

Hermes Trismegistus was considered to be the author of an ancient Greek text on theories (called "Hermetic") that identified astrology and alchemy as the means by which humankind could tap into the power of nature.

Fludd also believed that the philosophy of the Rosicrucian brotherhood (see page 56) was the natural development of Hermes Trismegistus. Fludd was not a member of the brotherhood, but believed that his theories and those of the brotherhood coincided on a number of key issues.

His theories about the connection between the Cosmos and humankind outlined in the superbly illustrated 1617 text *Ultiusque Cosmi Maloris Scilicet et Minoris Metaphysica, Physica atque Technica Historia* ("The History of the Macrocosm and Microcosm").

In this text, Fludd described the creation of the universe and the world, when a balance of light and dark was created. He believed that all things were created from the light of God, and that there was a unity or harmony between the macrocosm (the universe) and the microcosm (the human being). In particular, he thought that the microcosm was a reflection of the structure of the macrocosm, and vice versa.

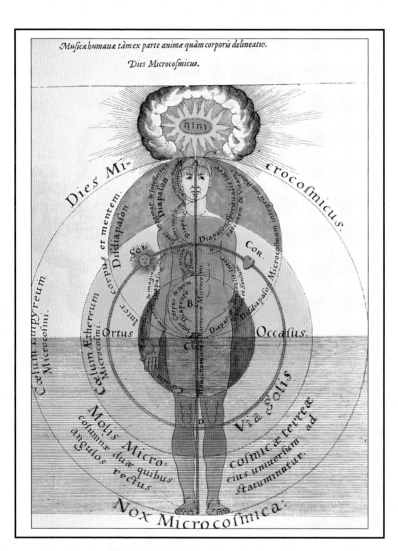

The three-fold man related to the planetary celestial harmonics.
From Robert Fludd's *Utriusque Cosmi Maioris*, 1617.

# COUNT SAINT-GERMAINE

ount Saint-Germaine came to the attention of the court of Louis XV in the mid-eighteenth century as an intriguing character who claimed immortality and was able to tell stories about events in history as if he had actually been there. He colorfully claimed to have chatted to such historical personages as the Queen of Sheba.

He stunned courtiers and King alike by refusing to partake of the sumptuous banquets of the court, claiming to survive on a secret elixir that gave him immortal life. However, it was believed that he dined exclusively on white food, such as chicken breast and oats.

His claims of immortality put him in the realm of the Merlin legend, where, like Merlin, he acquired a great deal of information that supposedly could not be amassed in one lifetime. He also traveled widely and was part of many of the major events of history.

Saint-Germaine tapped into the legend of the Philosopher's Stone in two ways. First, he intimated that he was the possessor of an elixir that gave him immortal life. Second, he gained a reputation for his alchemical prowess at transforming the common into the something of the highest quality. However, stories about Saint-Germaine focused less on metals than on the transformation of common and imperfect stones into diamonds and other precious stones.

He appeared at court as a well-dressed, extremely wealthy foreigner who wore magnificent jewellery. He became sought after for his many and varied skills, ranging from being ambidextrous to his legendary ability to recall a conversation a few days before with a courtier, or several hundreds of years earlier with Queen Cleopatra. Although he professed to be of the Catholic faith, Saint-Germaine was also said to have skills at clairvoyance and telepathy.

Being a gregarious and generous man, he delighted the French court with his gifts of supposedly precious gems and magical trinkets, such as a box in which an image would magically appear in the stone when it was brought close to fire. However, his fashionableness at court began to wane and he became embroiled in charges of treason, which led him to flee France.

Count Saint-Germaine was a shadowy and fascinating character, and historians have long debated his fantastic claims and the many stories about him. In the middle of the nineteenth century, an occultist who used the pen name Eliphas Lévi devoted a few pages to the activities of Saint-Germaine in *The History of Magic* (see pages 28–29). Levi declared that Saint-Germaine had actually been born in the late seventeenth century in Bohemia, the natural or adopted son of a member of the Rosicrucian brotherhood (see page 56).

It is believed that Saint-Germaine died in 1784 while under the patronage of Charles of Hesse in Germany. However,

his fame — or notoriety — continued. His claim of immortality persisted after his apparent death, as there were a number of alleged sightings of him after 1784.

The Count de Saint-Germaine born circa 1710, died 1784. Print after the original copperplate of 1783 by N Thomas, after the long-lost painting formerly in the von Urfe Collection.

# ELİPHAS LÉVİ

E liphas Lévi was the pen name of Alphonse Louis Constant, who came to prominence in the mid-nineteenth century as a writer and teacher of the occult, being particularly interested in the Kabbalah (see pages 118–119). So keen was his interest in this well-regarded Jewish system of magic that he created a pen name that was a Hebrew version of his first and second names.

Born in 1810 in poverty, Lévi showed promise, and studied to become a priest. However, his interest in the occult and his inability to stop himself from voicing his opinions led to his expulsion from the seminary at Saint-Sulpice. A meeting with a self-styled "prophet" named Ganneau strengthened his interest in the occult.

Interest in magic in the mid-nineteenth century had been inspired by Francis Barrett's *The Magus*, published in 1801 (see pages 84–85). Lévi's occults works, such as *The Doctrine and Ritual of Transcendental Magic* and *A History of Magic*, heightened this interest.

Lévi set out a number of his beliefs in *Transcendental Magic*, affirming the existence of a "potent and real Magic," which could impart superhuman powers. He identified the source of this "Magic" as the understanding of Nature, which was handed down from the ancient Magi. The Magi were the possessors of the secrets of nature, in particular the understanding of the mystical power of fire. They have sometimes been referred to as an ancient group of Wizards.

Levi not only wrote about magic; he practiced it as well. He tried to call up the spirit of one of the ancient world's most celebrated Wizards, Apollonius of Tyana (now part of Turkey). Lévi described Apollonius as a great personality whose history was "epoch-making in the annals of Magic."

Apollonius was believed to have lived in the second century AD, and had the reputation of being a prophet and a healer able to banish pestilence from whole towns. When he fell foul of Emperor Severus, Apollonius was brought to trial, but in a spectacular final gesture he vanished from the courtroom.

Lévi prepared himself for the ritual of calling up the spirit of Apollonius by first eating only vegetarian meals and then fasting, as well as by meditating on the ancient Wizard. During the twelve-hour ritual Lévi was successful in conjuring a "shadow" just after experiencing an intense feeling of coldness. Although uncertain whether he had in fact called up Apollonius, Lévi continued to conduct rituals, and claimed he had been successful in contacting the Wizard during these rituals.

Lévi died in 1875, leaving a legacy of magical thoughts and ideas, which was later taken up by the Hermetic Order of the Golden Dawn (see pages 58–59). Aleister Crowley (see pages 30–31), a Wizard who was notorious in the late nineteenth and early twentieth centuries and who was born in the year of Lévi's death, believed that he was the reincarnation of Lévi.

## WIZARDLY QUOTE

*Magic, therefore, combines in a single science that which is most certain in philosophy, which is eternal and infallible in religion. It reconciles perfectly and incontestably those two terms, so opposed on the first view — faith and reason, science and belief, authority and liberty. It furnishes the human mind with an instrument of philosophical and religious certitude as exact as mathematics, and even accounting for the infallibility of mathematics themselves.*
*Eliphas Lévi, in* The History of Magic *(translated by A.E. Waite)*

# ALEISTER CROWLEY

An insatiable appetite for knowledge, married to an equally
voracious lust for sex, drugs and the experience of other
bodily pleasures, colored the magical career of this
important but deeply troubled Wizard of the late nineteenth and
early twentieth centuries.

Born in 1875, the same year that Eliphas Lévi died, Crowley
strongly believed that he had been a Wizard in previous
lifetimes, an Egyptian priest, Lévi (see pages 28–29), and Count
Alessandro Cagliostro, who was a controversial Wizardly figure
in the eighteenth century, believed at the time to hold the secret
of the Philosopher's Stone.

Crowley's early career in the occult began gradually. He
indulged in his interest in the darker aspects of the occult, finally
coming to the conclusion that he should make magic his
vocation. He joined the Hermetic Order of the Golden Dawn
(see pages 58–59), but soon argued with various members of the
Order, including its head, Samuel Liddell MacGregor Mathers.

Expelled from the Order, Crowley traveled widely and was
able to study the Kabbalah (see pages 118–119), Buddhism,
Egyptian occultism, and Enochian magic. He believed that he
was also the reincarnation of Edward Kelly (see pages 22–23).

Crowley married Rose Kelly, who was believed to be the
channel of Crowley's guardian angel, an entity called Aiwass.

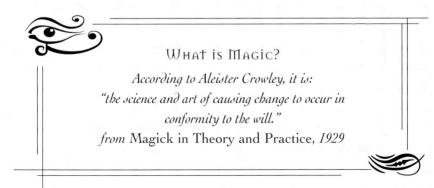

### What is Magic?

*According to Aleister Crowley, it is:*
*"the science and art of causing change to occur in*
*conformity to the will."*
from Magick in Theory and Practice, *1929*

This entity played a crucial role in dictating one of Crowley's most important published texts, *The Book of the Law*. In this text, the occult community was first introduced to what was referred to as the Law of Thelema. *Thelema* is a Greek word meaning will.

This "Law," which is believed by some to be one of Crowley's most major contributions to current magical thinking, states: "Do what Thou Wilt shall be the whole of the Law." Failure to adhere strictly to this Law came to be Crowley's undoing. He established The Abbey of Thelema in Sicily in 1920, based on Rabelais's imaginary Abbey of Thélème; both the real and the fictional "order" degenerated into self-indulgence.

Although Crowley was able to establish that magic could come about when one followed one's true will or path through life, he did not have the discipline to keep to his own true will or path. He was deflected by the distractions of an overactive and over-stimulated mind.

After expulsion from the Golden Dawn in 1900, Crowley was not involved with another organized group until 1911, when he joined the Ordo Templi Orientis (OTO), a group established in Germany in 1902. One of the OTO's principal premises was that ritual sex was a powerful way of linking with the divine within. Crowley was instrumental in setting up an English branch of the Order and he rewrote many of their rituals, basing new ceremonies on *The Book of the Law*. Crowley reveled in controversy and in depictions of himself in the press as "The Great Beast" and "The Wickedest Man in the World," but he was plagued by heroin addiction and poor health. He died in relative poverty and obscurity in 1949.

Aleister Crowley: writer, artist, and occultist, who delighted in being known as "the Great Beast."

# GERALD GARDNER

G erald Gardner was primarily responsible for reviving an interest in Witchcraft in mid-twentieth-century England. This revival was set against the repeal of the *Witchcraft Act 1735* and the publication of *The Great Beast*, a biography of Aleister Crowley (see pages 30–31) by John Symonds.

Gardner was very familiar with Crowley's magical works, and encapsulated some of the magical concepts first raised by Crowley in a codified version of what a Witch/Wizard did in the twentieth century. He also presented a version of Witchcraft that he believed was derived from pre-Christian Pagan religion and folklore. In particular, Gardner was instrumental in helping to make it clear that Witchcraft had nothing at all to do with the Devil of the Christian mythos.

While honing his magical beliefs, and with the aid of a small band of friends and magical partners, including Doreen Valiente, Gardner developed a *Book of Shadows*, which contained rituals, spells and other notes that captured the spirit of a religious and magical system. This in time gave rise to a coherent Witchcraft movement, now known as Wicca.

Gardner's *Book of Shadows* was the primary "source" used in his published books, including *Witchcraft Today*, which was published in 1954. In these books Gardner outlined the beliefs of those who practice magic, and gave his theories about the start and development of Witchcraft, asserting the existence of a link going back as far as the Stone Age.

Gardner was very heavily influenced by Charles Godfrey Leland, the author of *Aradia, the Gospel of the Witches* (1899), a book purporting to contain evidence of a goddess-oriented religion.

According to Gardner, Witches' beliefs included reincarnation and their practices encapsulated Goddess worship and a reverence of nature. Gardner's interest in folklore and Celtic

Portrait of Gerald Brousseau Gardner (1894–1964), esotericist and founder of a branch of Wicca, and founder of the Witchcraft museum at Castletown.

tradition filtered through his writings. He was particularly interested in balancing the energy of a God with that of a Goddess, since observations of nature show that in nearly all life forms there are both male and female aspects.

The supreme flowering of magic was, to Gardner, the performance of the Great Rite, where two consenting adults engage in a sexual union to raise energy, which can be channeled for a magical purpose.

Gardner also popularized the concept of working magical rituals skyclad. Skyclad means performing magical rituals in the nude. The reasoning was that clothes retain the energy of the everyday, which may get in the way of a spiritual ritual. This and many other of Gardner's ideas were adopted in the practice of white magic, and led a number of psychically sensitive people to study and become Witches — male "Gardnerian" Witches do not refer to themselves as Wizards but are sometimes called, depending on the ritual, High Priests.

# ALEXANDER SANDERS

Alexander Sanders was a founder of his own branch of Wicca.

Where Gerald Gardner (see pages 32–33) integrated some of Aleister Crowley's magical ideas and developed in the 1950s an esoteric system that was fundamentally down to earth, Alex Sanders's style in the 1960s was closer to Crowley's flair for showmanship and dramatic ceremony. Alexander Sanders, in the fertile atmosphere of the 1960s, was very successful at creating the publicity necessary to attract a greater number of people to Witchcraft (known as Wicca, or The Craft), and helped them discover the true precepts of Witchcraft.

Following Gardner's lead in giving his brand of Witchcraft a coherent and unbroken lineage, Sanders claimed to have been initiated as a Witch by his grandmother, who was a hereditary Witch. The British press also gleefully publicized the claim that

he was "King of the Witches," the number of Witches in Britain reputedly exceeding 1,000 in the 1960s. Like Gardner before him, Sander had a fondness for publicity that often left him vulnerable to his critics. Irrespective of his theatricality and the publicity generated by the press, however, Sanders was strongly devoted to the study of Witchcraft, and unstintingly shared his knowledge with those he felt were sincere in their beliefs.

The publicity generated by Sanders certainly did contribute to the rapid growth of the Witchcraft movement. Like Gardner, Sanders believed in conducting initiations for those interested in undertaking a study of Witchcraft, provided that they were over the age of 18 and willing to commit themselves to this study. Both Gardnerian and Alexandrian versions of Witchcraft require initiation. Both have three degrees, each of which requires the development of a certain level of knowledge and self-awareness.

Those initiated by Sanders followed an Alexandrian path of Witchcraft. Current Alexandrian Witches have been initiated by these earlier initiates, or have joined a coven or small group who follow this path of Witchcraft. The essential elements of this path appear to have been borrowed from Gardner, particularly a reverence for nature and a balance between God and Goddess energies in ritual. Sanders also borrowed freely from the writings of Eliphas Lévi (see pages 28–29).

Sanders had genuine psychic abilities and a sensitivity that he used in devising rituals. He also did healing work, predominantly with the help of a channeled familiar called Michael.

Sanders also added a few more flourishes in the ritual ceremony, borrowing from the ceremonial magic of ancient Wizards. He incorporated elements of the Kabbalah (see pages 118–119), Egyptian magic, and the magic of a Jewish Mage who lived in the mid-fourteenth and fifteenth centuries called Abramelin. He continued the tradition of skyclad rituals, but, curiously, excepted himself, often appearing dramatically robed in the midst of a skyclad coven.

# OBERON ZELL-RAVENHEART

Oberon Zell-Ravenheart, like many Wizards before him, has an insatiable lust for knowledge and life. With an active and inquiring mind, he has studied in many areas, having academic degrees in sociology, anthropology, clinical psychology and theology.

During these studies, Zell-Ravenheart has sought deeper knowledge, studying the occult and the practices of many esoteric groups, and becoming an initiate in a number of different magical traditions. For instance, he is an ordained Priest of the Earth-Mother, Gaia, an initiate in the Egyptian Church of the Eternal Source, and a Priest in the Fellowship of Isis.

Unlike many celebrated Wizards before him, Zell-Ravenheart has not worked in isolation, but has been instrumental in gathering like-minded individuals to Pagan spirituality. One of his major contributions to twentieth-century Pagan spirituality has been the co-founding of the Church of All Worlds in 1962, inspired by Robert A. Heinlein's 1961 science-fiction novel *Stranger in a Strange Land*.

Zell-Ravenheart is a Wizard who is able not only to study and perceive the patterns of nature and energy flows, but also to use this knowledge for the betterment of his own life and that of the various communities gathered around him. He has also been instrumental in disseminating this knowledge through the publication of an influential Pagan magazine called *Green Egg* (first published in 1968).

Zell-Ravenheart has the discipline of mind, the gregarious nature and the depth of understanding of human beings to put him into the category of a Merlin style of Wizard (see pages 12–13).

At certain times, Zell-Ravenheart has served his community in what he describes as "the traditional capacity of a rural Wizard." He has been active in creating and leading rituals to take care of

the community's spiritual needs, those that mark the change of the seasons and the important events of life, such as initiations, special rites of passage, handfastings (Pagan rituals akin to marriages) and baby blessings, and other rituals, such as protections, house blessings and exorcisms.

His own reverence of nature led Zell-Ravenheart to formulate and publish a "theology of deep ecology" in 1970, which came to be known as *The Gaia Thesis*. Zell-Ravenheart comments that the thesis "first proposed the idea of viewing our entire planetary biosphere as a single vast living organism, with humankind being just one part of an integrated and interconnected living system." He equated this planetary being with the ancient concept of Mother Earth – an important premise subsequently adopted by many ecological movements.

With his wife and soul mate, Morning Glory, Zell-Ravenheart also founded the Ecosophical Research Association, researching arcane lore and ancient legends. This led to their developing their "Living Unicorn Project:" from 1980 to 1984 they bred traditional, Renaissance-style unicorns to "herald the return of Magick and the dawn of a new Golden Age."

# CHAPTER 2
# THE WIZARD'S WORLD

## INTRODUCTION: A WORLD OF MANY BELIEFS

A s in any profession or industry, there are many types of Wizards. A number of the Wizards discussed in the previous chapter were the loners who broke new ground and tried to communicate new ideas or discoveries to the world, with some claiming they gained their information from a variety of sources, including contact with spirits from other planes of existence.

These types of Wizards tend to be the scholars, the authors, and the seekers of deeper knowledge that explains or attempts to explain our existence and our connection with a greater power. They have also tried to understand the patterns of nature, and some have even been tempted to theorize or adopt theories that systematized the various levels of existence. This type of Wizard, ranging from Agrippa to Alex Sanders, has often been attracted to Ceremonial Magic (see pages 120–121) or High Magic.

High Magic incorporates various systems of magic, such as the Kabbalah (see pages 118–119), astrology (see pages 104–107), and numerology (see pages 116–117). High Magic can also be described as magic used to gain insight into yourself and the world around you.

When a Wizard uses his magical knowledge to help people who approach him with their everyday problems, he is said to be practicing Low Magic. Helping people gain insight into their futures, find their true love, gain or protect their fortune or possessions, and exorcize bad spirits from their home, despite the worthiness of these aims, is generally classed as Low Magic.

Practitioners of high magic have been drawn to ancient systems of magic and, in particular, the magic of ancient Egypt (see pages 40–43). These ancient systems of magic, particularly the Egyptian, were very influential in the formation of nineteenth-century societies that attracted a number of Wizards to their ranks, particularly the Hermetic Order of the Golden Dawn (see pages 58–59).

Other occult groups and orders, such as the Druids (see pages 44–47), the Freemasons (see pages 54–55), and the Rosicrucians (see page 56), who had their beginnings in the mists of time, also flourished in the nineteenth century. Their popularity was no doubt partly in response to the Industrial Revolution, where the grimness of a new, faster moving industrial upheaval generated nostalgia for a soulful, romantic existence.

Similarly, the rapid development of technological breakthroughs in the twentieth and the twenty-first centuries has led a number of modern Witches and Wizards to explore tribal or village magic, seeking a sense of community and finding inspiration in the role of the shaman in traditional societies, such as those of the Native Americans (see pages 48–53).

However, the advances in technology have also helped modern Witches and Wizards, by enabling the fast communication of ideas, and easier access to arcane and previously difficult to obtain knowledge. Inspiration has also come from forms of modern-day entertainment — publishing, movies, videos, DVDs and the Internet have come to offer more fuel to the creative Wizard.

# WIZARDS OF ANCIENT EGYPT

## ANCIENT EGYPT: THE MOTHER OF MAGICIANS

In Egypt, magic was a way of life. Priests looked after the daily rituals believed to be needed for ushering in the new day and keeping the seasonal balance before and after the flooding of the Nile; magicians fulfilled another role.

All Egyptians, ranging from the farmer to the pharaoh, approached Wizards to find out their fate and the fate of their loved ones, and to find ways of protecting themselves from an uncomfortable life. The ancient Egyptians believed that magic was a gift from the creator to help ward off the blows of fate.

Wizards were able to practice clairvoyance and to make amulets and talismans after conducting certain rituals. These rituals were designed to help Wizards perform the magic correctly. The rituals were contained in papyruses that are now popularly known as *The Book of the Dead*. This "Book" is also known in ancient Egyptian as *Pert em Hru*, which can be roughly translated as "Coming into the Light."

Words were very important magical tools for ancient Egyptian Wizards. The right words were believed to have the power to control a variety of supernatural entities, even certain Gods or Goddesses. Reciting the incantations could supposedly bring the things that the Wizard was thinking of into reality. It was also believed that by saying the name of the object and fueling the word with the Wizard's will the object would actually appear.

To become a Wizard in ancient Egypt, a postulant needed to learn visualization skills. The Wizard also had to be adept at

astral traveling, a practice where a person can travel in spirit to various places while his or her physical body remains at rest elsewhere.

There were a number of levels that a Wizard in Ancient Egypt could attain in his magical development, ending in the level of Master of the Universe, where the Wizard was able to have power over the events of not only his life but also his rebirth. Such a high ranking Wizard would be able to move from reincarnation to reincarnation without losing track of what he had learnt in previous lives.

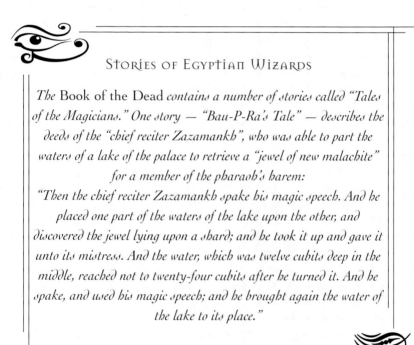

### Stories of Egyptian Wizards

*The* Book of the Dead *contains a number of stories called "Tales of the Magicians." One story — "Bau-P-Ra's Tale" — describes the deeds of the "chief reciter Zazamankh", who was able to part the waters of a lake of the palace to retrieve a "jewel of new malachite" for a member of the pharaoh's harem:*
*"Then the chief reciter Zazamankh spake his magic speech. And he placed one part of the waters of the lake upon the other, and discovered the jewel lying upon a shard; and he took it up and gave it unto its mistress. And the water, which was twelve cubits deep in the middle, reached not to twenty-four cubits after he turned it. And he spake, and used his magic speech; and he brought again the water of the lake to its place."*

## A SPECIAL EGYPTIAN SPELL FOR CONTROLLING CHAOS

ythological stories, such as the creation of the Cosmos, often provide a framework for ancient Egyptian spells. According to Egyptian myth, heka, or magic, was used to create a world out of the swirling chaos overseen by the great Egyptian serpent God Apep.

For this special spell to eliminate chaos from your life, collect the following simple ingredients:

- a lump of clay;
- a piece of black cloth; and
- a stem of corn.

At dusk, take the lump of clay and fashion it into a long coil to represent a serpent, and cut the kernels from your corncob, discarding or saving them. Find a place in your home or your garden where you feel safe and where you will not be disturbed.

Near the edge of your space, place the serpent at your feet. Take half a step back and draw a circle around you, either with a stick or through visualization, making it large enough so you can sit down comfortably inside it. This circle will protect you from negative forces. When seated, place the corn stem near your feet and the black cloth by your side.

Imagine that the space within the circle is the primeval mound — the first piece of land that the Egyptians believed emerged from the dark watery chaos called the Nun. Focus on the corncob. This is the symbol of new life.

Imagine a white light emanating from the corncob. Say the following words:

*Let the power of Maat, Goddess of justice, truth and harmony, rule in my new life, giving me peace, the power of creativity and the joy of living.*

Imagine a healing white light surrounding you. Beyond your circle, darkness is swirling. This is your personal Nun — all the unhappiness and negative emotions that you have been

The Egyptian cat-goddess, Bast, slaying the serpent-demon Apep. In the
background, the Persea tree.

experiencing — and home of the God of chaos, Apep. Through
your protective white light, see the darkness being sucked into
the little clay image. Say the following words:

*Serpent God of chaos and disorder, your true name is Apep.*
*As I know your true name, you can no longer hurt me*
*with your destructive forces. Stay within yourimage. You*
*no longer have the power to hurt me and those that I love.*

When you feel ready, imagine the white light around you
reentering the corn stem. Imagine that your circle is now open,
or erase it if you have inscribed it physically. Pick up the clay
serpent image with your black cloth and wrap it up carefully.
This will keep the destructive energy confined. Keep the corn
stem with you until you have a chance to take the clay image to
a river, stream or the sea. Take the image out of the black cloth
and throw it away from you, imagining that the chaos has
completely left your life.

# THE DRUIDS OF ANCIENT CELTIC BRITAIN

## Ancient Druidic Traditions

The word "Druid" is a Gaelic word that refers to the knowledge of the oak tree. Indeed, the ancient Druids were renowned for many skills that derived from their profound knowledge of the cycles of nature, the knowledge of the omens encoded in the movements of animals, fish and birds, and their understanding of the healing properties of herbs.

The Druids were even accredited with the ability to transform people into various creatures, such as eagles, wolfhounds and salmon. The Druids themselves could also "shapeshift" — change their outer shape by will.

It is believed that there were Druids as far back as the fifth century BC. Much of their ritual and knowledge was kept secret. Their wisdom was transmitted orally through poetry and song rather than through the written word. Their beliefs and powers have come down to us through secondary accounts, in particular the writings of Roman and Greek travelers and epic poems transcribed by early monks.

The Druids practiced astronomy, studying the stars and their movements. It was believed, during a revival of interest in the Druids in the sixteenth and seventeenth centuries, that Stonehenge was constructed by the Druids, but this has been since discredited, as the stones predate the Druids.

However, the Druids were believed to have used Stonehenge to chart the change of the seasons. They were steadfast in observing the celebration of important seasonal festivals,

including those that marked the summer and winter solstices, as well as the autumnal and vernal equinoxes.

Not only did the Druids allegedly have the power to forecast the weather; stories abounded of their ability to conjure dense fogs, showers and heavy snowfalls — particularly useful for hampering the activities of Christian missionaries.

Their knowledge of nature and their ability to make powerful amulets and to interpret dreams were venerated by the ancient Celts, who sought their divinatory skills. However, rather horrific stories emerged about the different ways Druids would perform their divinatory practices.

By the time of the invasion of Britain by the Romans in the first century AD, grisly accounts of the practices were given by the Romans, including Julius Caesar himself. Stories were told of the burning of animal and human sacrifices in wicker cages shaped like a man. This gave Caesar the opportunity for suppressing Druidic practices. Current historians have now called these stories into question.

The Ancient Order of Druids had evolved by the end of the eighteenth century, and various Druidic societies developed in both Britain and North America.

## A Battle Between Ancient Druids

*One Druid was employed by a rebel leader in southwest Ireland to cast a spell over a community led by the King of Munster. The community experienced a severe drought that led to the death of many people, animals and crops. The King of Munster sought and found a more powerful Druid, who was able to break the enchanted drought by casting a spear into the ground. At the very spot where his spear pierced the ground, a bubbling spring of water emerged, saving the people loyal to the King of Munster.*

## Celtic spells and legends

The Druids took great pride in being able not only to observe and understand the energies shifts of nature, but also to blend into their surroundings, becoming effectively invisible. The Druid seeking invisibility would intone the following incantation:

*A magic cloud I put on thee,*
*From dog, from cat,*
*From cow, from horse,*
*From man, from woman,*
*From young man, from maiden,*
*And from little child.*
*Till I again return.*

This incantation and other Celtic spells were called "fath-fith" or "fith-fath," meaning "words of magic." As the Druids did not write any of their magical practices, they remembered the magical words and procedures in the form of poems, some of which have become part of Celtic folklore. Irish bards were thought to have been the main group of people responsible for retaining Druidic knowledge.

It is believed that there were three types of Druids. The highest level were accorded the title of Druid but eventually all levels came to be known as Druids. On the lowest level were the *vates*, who were gifted at divination, while the middle level was occupied by the bards, who had the ability to memorize enormous screeds of sacred lore.

Druids, like most Wizards, were keen to find shortcuts to acquiring supernatural knowledge and universal wisdom. One way of doing so was by watching a hazelnut tree, one of the types of trees held sacred by the Wizards. If the hazelnuts fell from the tree into a stream and were eaten by a salmon, a Druid would be very keen to catch that salmon and eat its flesh.

It is believed that hazelnuts had the power to convey knowledge about everything in the world. According to legend, a salmon that had eaten a hazelnut that had fallen into the water from the sacred tree was caught and cooked by Finn MacCoul, the leader of the Fenians (a tribe from the Old Celtic histories of the Invasions). After eating the fish he was reputed to have the power to heal any wound or disease by giving the victim a drink from his cupped hands.

Finn MacCoul, while cooking the salmon, touched a blister forming on its side from the heat. Burning his thumb on the fish, the legendary leader hurriedly put it into his mouth and was astonished to find that he had been granted supernatural sight. This and other legends about the "Salmon of Knowledge" or *Eo Feasa* made it a very desirable catch for the Druids.

Druids were approached to help people protect themselves from enchantment and the evil eye. It was believed that an object made from iron could provide protection from evil. An iron pin attached to a hat or a small amount of iron sewn into a seam in a piece of clothing was considered sufficient to protect the wearer from evil intentions. An iron horseshoe was also nailed up over the door with the ends pointing up. It was considered that the best horseshoe for protection was one cast from the hind leg of a gray mare.

# NATIVE AMERICAN SHAMANS

### THE SHAMANIC PATH

The strong connection between the shaman, his natural environment and the spirit world has attracted many Wizards and Witches who practice modern-day magic. Both shamanism and modern-day magic exhibit a belief in the benefit of worshiping and understanding nature, and many aspects of shamanism have been incorporated in a wide range of modern magical systems.

The traditions of Native American Indian shamans vary from tribe to tribe and need to be viewed in the context of the particular circumstances affecting the main crops of the tribe and the seasonal changes in the region they occupy. Despite such variables, it was common ground that shamans were the protectors of the village, helping their community to survive.

As with any group of people living on the land, the weather was one of the most important forces, able to give or take life. Shamans, using whatever tools and creatures were around them, had the gift to forecast the weather or to conduct rituals where the Gods were asked to bless the crop or send rain.

Who becomes a shaman? It is believed that certain people are "called" to become shamans by the spirits, frequently after a life-threatening illness or accident. Sometimes, too, a person experiences dreams that foretell an impending life-threatening trial and is given the option to follow the shaman's path. If that person does not wish to follow the path, he or she will often find that the illness worsens and a return to life is not allowed.

Once a person has been coaxed or coerced into becoming a shaman, he or she will find a number of the "tools" will magically appear or be found in strange places. These tools usually consist of a drum, rattle, furs, claws, and dreamcatchers. The shaman's powers are often presented to him or her through visions.

Because of their ability to commune with the spirit world, shamans are generally both highly respected and feared. Within the village hierarchy, shamans were the loners who helped the community by being able to move between the material and the spirit worlds. Consequently, shamans received help not from the tribe but from their spirit guides who, it was believed, helped them assess how to deal with the various problems of their tribe.

These guides often take the form of particular animals, called power animals. They are on the lowest astral plane and are the easiest for a shaman to access.

It is widely believed that there are three levels in the astral world. The next level consists of the ancestors of members of the tribe, and on the upper level of spirits are teachers who can help the shaman understand deeply the signs of human behavior and the omens of weather changes.

A ceremony invoking the Great Spirit.

THE WIZARD'S WORLD

## Making a Dreamcatcher

### WHAT IS A DREAMCATCHER?

A dreamcatcher is an imitation of a spider's web, woven onto a wooden or metal frame. Pliable wood can be formed into a circle that is generally the size of a person's hand. In traditional dreamcatchers, a commercial hoop of the same size can also be used. The web within the circle was woven from animal sinew (such as that of a deer), plant fiber, or red colored yarn. The web can be decorated with gems at the four compass points to invoke the elements of Air, Fire, Water, and Earth.

| Compass directions | Corresponding elements | Corresponding gems |
|---|---|---|
| North | Earth | Obsidian, Jet |
| South | Fire | Topaz, Ruby |
| East | Air | Lapis lazuli, Quartz crystal (clear) |
| West | Water | Turquoise, Moonstone |

It is important that the web has a hole in the middle and that the string left over from making the web is securely knotted and decorated with a few beads, feathers or small metal images of animals. In some traditions, a feather would decorate the center of the web, with an eagle feather being used for a boy and an owl feather for a girl. The decorated feather should hang freely past the bottom of the dreamcatcher. The web can be woven in a number of different designs, depending on the size of the frame, with the pattern usually built up by the repetition of a basic "stitch."

### THE DREAMCATCHER LEGEND

In traditional Native American folklore, the dreamcatcher was hung over the head of a loved one's bed. Its purpose was to entangle evil dreams — dreams distracting or unimportant to the sleeper — within the dreamcatcher's web and allow only

good dreams to trickle down the web through the beads and feathers to the head of the sleeping child or adult.

Dreamcatchers for children are made of fragile materials, such as willow, grapevine or cedar, to underline the fact that childhood is a temporary state. Dreamcatchers for adults are usually made from more permanent materials, such as a metal hoop covered with a leather thong.

It is believed that the evil dreams will swirl hopelessly around the web until the rays of the early morning sun destroyed them. A dreamcatcher might not take away all the nightmares if the disturbing images are intended to provide an important message to the sleeping person.

To the Native Americans, dreams are a particularly important connection with the spirit world, special communications between human beings and their spirit guides, power animals and nature spirits. They are taken very seriously as solutions to any crises in a person's spiritual or material development. The visions are considered sacred.

WHAT YOU WILL NEED TO MAKE YOUR DREAMCATCHER
For your frame you may wish to purchase a commercial hoop, such as an embroidery frame, or make your frame from 2 to 6 feet (0.6 to 2 meters) of a thin, pliant wood, such as willow or grapevine, soaked in water until the wood feels easy to bend.

For your web, you will need strong, thin string, such as a leather thong, twine, or even a colored silk thread. You will need between 4 and 16 feet (1.2 to 5 meters) of string.

Next, collect the animal symbols, semi-precious stones, beads, and feathers (those you find yourself or simulated feathers from a craft store) that you wish to use to decorate your dreamcatcher. Make sure that the thread you have chosen for your web passes easily through the holes in the beads.

## MAKING A DREAMCATCHER FRAME

If you are making a dreamcatcher for a child, measure the span of the child's hand and use that as a guide to the size of the dreamcatcher. As a child's dreamcatcher should be impermanent, consider making the frame rather than purchasing it.

To make the circular frame, bend your wooden branch to form a small circle, intertwining the ends of the branch back into the frame to strengthen the circle. If you are using delicate threads for your web, secure the circle by looping copper or silver wire a number of times around the ends of the branches and pulling tight. If you are using strong, hardy string for your web, use it to tie the branches together. You may wish to knot a loop at the point where the branches overlap so that you can hang your dreamcatcher from the loop when it is completed.

## WEAVING THE WEB

The web is woven by using the same looping stitch, spaced evenly about 2 inches (5 cm) apart on the frame. Secure the thread at the top of the frame and loop the thread loosely over the frame, and then over the thread, to create a loop. Continue this stitch all the way around the frame, making sure that the tension of the thread is taut — but not too tight, as it may warp the frame.

When you have come full circle around the frame, you will be ready to start the first round of the web. From the last stitch on the frame, make your next loop in the middle of the first stitch on the frame. Continue this stitch in the middle of all the stitches on the frame, pulling the thread so that you create a triangle.

Continue this stitch until the hole in the middle of the frame is almost closed. You should have some string left, and onto this you can tie your animal symbol or thread your beads or feather. Hang this dreamcatcher over your bed for a restful night's sleep.

IXOS

Images to decorate the middle of your web

**Frog** – *happiness*, **Turtle** – *health*, **Rabbit** – *peace*, **Bear** – *protection*,
**Eagle** – *better communication*, **Horse** – *prosperity*

# WIZARDS OF THE MODERN WORLD

### FREEMASONS

The Freemasons trace their beginnings to the masons who worked on the famous temple of King Solomon. Masons were essentially craftsmen who cut stone and prepared it for various building projects. Many master masons were akin to modern day architects, possessors of the knowledge of structure.

Legend has it that an architect or master builder by the name of Hiram Abiff, entrusted by Solomon with the building of the Temple, came by the happy notion of dividing his force of over 180,000 craftsmen according to their skill and experience.

This was necessary because the job required an unprecedented number of itinerant workers to complete the job. Hiram's system ensured that the right people were given the right kind of work and were remunerated accordingly. There were three levels — the Apprentices, the Companions and the Masters — and each level was identified by the use of particular passwords and signs. On particularly large building projects, lodges were set up to interview incoming masons to ascertain whether the men had the suitable experience.

The word "freemason" was first recorded in London as early as 1375, and related to a prestigious group of men who had what then seemed the magical power to build large, powerful structures. Some believe that the Freemasons borrowed their emblems from a guild of masons who were working at the cathedral of Strasburg.

The Freemasons' handshake was an easy way of indicating
membership of the secret order.

Eventually, Freemasonry became open not only to masons but
also to men of good reputation, irrespective of their religion.
Eliphas Lévi described the fundamental basis of the Freemasons
in his *The History of Magic*, where he comments that:

*Truth is the object of their worship, and they represent truth*
*as light; they tolerate all forms of faith, profess one philosophy,*
*seek truth only, teach reality, and their plan is to lead all*
*human intelligence by gradual steps into the domain of reason.*

By the eighteenth century, Freemasonry's tenets of equality,
tolerance and brotherhood had attracted some of the most
enlightened and politically active men of the time, such as
George Washington, Benjamin Franklin, Voltaire and Wolfgang
Amadeus Mozart.

Freemasonry prospered in eighteenth-century England,
America and France, with lodges also established in other
European countries, such as Germany, Italy and Russia.

The Freemasons are still a secret society today, requiring
initiation rituals to be undertaken before a member first enters
the Society and subsequently, as the member progresses
through the different levels of the Society. Women were
excluded from the lodges until the late eighteenth century. In
1902, Co-Masonry was founded, a splinter group allowing
women as members.

## Rosicrucians

The Rosicrucian brotherhood or order was allegedly first established in fifteenth-century Germany. Its founder was a mysterious figure called Christian Rosenkreutz (literally translated as "Christian Rosycross"), who was a great healer, and also gained access, during a pilgrimage, to a book that held the secrets of the universe. With a group of men, he began an order called the Brothers of the Rosy Cross.

The name of the brotherhood is linked to important Christian symbols, respectively, the rose and the cross: they refer to the Virgin Mary and Christ. However, the beliefs of the Rosicrucians went beyond Christian theology, focusing on the occult arts, such as alchemy.

Some believed that the symbol of the rose and cross signifies the balance between the darkness of the cross and the spiritual transformation of the rose. The rose is apparently a reference to the alchemical term "ros," which in Latin means dew. Dew was believed to be the main ingredient in making the Philosopher's Stone (see pages 96–97).

By the seventeenth century the Rosicrucians were flourishing in England, Germany, the Netherlands and France, promoting peace and wisdom. However, in France the Rosicrucians attracted the hostility of the Catholic Church, which alleged that the Rosicrucians were making pacts with the Devil that gave them the power to speak with eloquence and persuasiveness.

The Rosicrucians were believed to have magical powers, which were developed by working through various grades. Their beliefs and membership remained secret, but they were reputed to have the ability to make the Philosopher's Stone, as they were believed to have understood the deepest secrets of natural magic.

The Rosy-cross of the early Rosicrucians: vignette from Joachim Frizius
*Summum Bonum*, 1629.

## Hermetic Order of the Golden Dawn

In nineteenth-century England, interest in the occult culminated in the establishment in 1888 of the Hermetic Order of the Golden Dawn. Although it lasted only until the beginning of the twentieth century, the Order attracted a number of prominent intellectuals who sought to obtain control of their personal power by tapping into the energy of the universe.

The Order was said to have its origins in an eighteenth-century German occult order that followed the magical traditions of Greece and Rome. This interest in the magical traditions of the West was possibly a reaction to the interest in Eastern philosophies shown by another influential order of the nineteenth century — the Theosophical Society.

Hermes was the Greek God of universal wisdom. He had associations with magic, sacred writings, astrology, philosophy, and alchemy. His qualities correspond closely with those of the Egyptian God Thoth. As a result, an Egyptian theme and occult traditions were adopted by the Order in their ceremonies, decorations and ritual garb.

The Order was founded by a group of like-minded men fascinated by the occult, and included Dr William Wynn Westcott and his protégé Samuel Liddell MacGregor Mathers. Both men had a long-term attraction to the occult and were members of a number of other secret societies, such as the the Rosicrucians (see page 56) and the Hermetic Society, and both were also Freemasons (see pages 54–55).

The combination of this group's interests and discoveries, such as Dr Westcott's studies in occult structures, Mathers's ability to bring theory into practice, and another member's discovery of apparently older initiation rituals, led to the development of the Order, commonly referred to as the Golden Dawn. A temple, called the Isis–Urania Temple, was established in London, and eventually Mathers established another in Paris.

Members, who included prominent occultist Aleister Crowley (see pages 30–31) and poet William Butler Yeats, were attracted to the Order's scholarly approach to Western magical knowledge. The Golden Dawn trained its members in various magical systems and teachings and conducted rituals to illustrate the workings of magic. The Order was a secret one and could only be joined through sponsorship and through participation in an initiation ritual. Several levels of progress through the Order were also devised.

The occult practices that evolved in the Order were a combination of the Kabbalah (see pages 118–119), the angelic Enochian language and rituals of Dr John Dee and Edward Kelly (see pages 22–23), the *Key of Solomon* grimoire (see page 86) and the magic of Abramelin, a fifteenth-century German sage who was interested in many forms of magic, including commanding the spirits.

Mathers translated the French version of the original Hebrew text supposedly written by Abramelin in 1458, called *The Sacred Magic of Abramelin the Mage*. He also translated and edited the famous grimoire *The Key of Solomon the King*.

Eventually the Golden Dawn became prey to schisms and infighting, with Aleister Crowley at first Mathers's ally and later his enemy. The pair allegedly engaged in psychic warfare with each other until they were both expelled from the Order in about 1900. The Golden Dawn splintered into a number of factions, whose practices were eventually subsumed — by the mid-twentieth century — by the Ceremonial Magic, Witchcraft and Pagan movements.

# Chapter 3
# A Wizard's Tools

## introduction: magical tools and the power of the elements

Magician with dividers, squaring the circle, symbolic of the magical operation
that brings spirit (circle) into matter (square).

The magical tools of the Wizards were as varied as the Wizards themselves. However, in the pursuit of both High Magic (gaining higher knowledge by understanding ourselves and the world around us) and Low Magic (applying this knowledge to the practical concerns of the material world), there is one common thread: the belief that four elements called Earth, Air, Fire and Water make up every thing in this world.

It was believed by many ancient civilizations that all knowledge is encoded in these elements and that we are linked both physically and psychically to the world's powerful source of energy because we too are made up of these elements.

In magic, this belief is often manifested in the tools that Wizards use to conduct their High Magic rituals and to fuel their Low Magic spellcraft. There are four important tools for a Wizard; each one represents one of the elements.

| *Element* | *Corresponding tool* |
|---|---|
| Earth | Pentacle or stone disc |
| Air | Athame (a double-edged knife) or incense burner |
| Fire | Wand or candle |
| Water | Chalice or bowl of water |

To create magic in your life and to empower your spells and any other magical work, it is important that you are also balanced in terms of the elements. A true Wizard will dedicate his life to attaining the balance of the four elements because when he attains this balance, he will then be a proper vessel for the flow of magical energy that will strengthen his work.

There are many techniques for achieving this internal, elemental balance. One way is to gain equal strength in the body (represented by the Earth element), the intellect (represented by the Air element), the will (represented the Fire element) and the emotions (represented by the Water element).

Other ways of achieving balance or acquiring the power to perform magic are often described in magical texts or grimoires (see pages 84–87); many Wizards also keep their own journals and records of their magical progress and development (see pages 88–89) to assess the success or otherwise of their magic.

The Wizard would also take the time to make his own tools (see pages 62–67), or would commission a craftsperson to make the objects to the Wizard's special design. With these tools, the Wizard would be able to make other important magical preparations, such as potions (see pages 68–69), talismans (see pages 70–79), and amulets (see pages 80–83).

# THE BASIC TOOLS

## THE POWER OF A WIZARD'S WAND

There are four important tools that most Wizards would be lost without — a wand, a crystal ball, an athame (a double-edged knife) and a chalice. These basic magical tools are used in virtually all High Magic ceremonies and for many Low Magic spells and other magical practices.

Probably the most famous magical tool associated with the Wizard is the wand (see pages 64–65). The Wizard's wand is a symbol of his will and his ability to direct his magical power toward a particular purpose. Magical wands are made from wood, with various traditions preferring the timber of a particular tree. Some magical traditions prefer to use the wood of an ash, rowan or hawthorn tree.

The Druids used hawthorn and rowan, but preferred their wands and staffs to be made out of the wood of the yew tree. Although oak was a sacred tree to the Druids, they did not use its wood to make their magical tools, choosing instead to hold some of their ceremonies within groves of oak trees.

Legends abound concerning the power of a Wizard's wand. If a person were struck with a Druidic wand, it was believed that the receiver of the blow could be transformed into an animal, such as a pig or a wolfhound, or turned invisible.

The wand was believed to be able to advise its owner whether someone was telling the truth. In one tradition it was thought that a person who stepped over the Wizard's wand could not resist telling the truth in response to a question put by the Wizard. This was one way in which a Wizard could apparently tell whether a woman was still a virgin.

To dedicate a new wand for magical purposes, the Wizard would light a number of candles on his altar and set a fire blazing in his nearby hearth. He would allow the flame in the hearth to rise, while holding out his hands to feel the intense heat and power infusing his hands. He would then pick up the wand and direct the power from his hands into the wood of the wand, imbuing it with life and energy. He would then say the following words:

> *Fire is Fire,*
> *Fire is will*
> *Fire is my tool*
> *Fire is my wand*
> *I am Fire!*

The Wizard would then take his wand and bless it with the other three elements. This he would do by passing the wand over a bowl of water and then over a stick of burning incense to bless it with the elements of water and air respectively. To consecrate the wand to the element of earth, the Wizard would then either sprinkle salt over the wand or bury it briefly in sacred ground.

Once fully consecrated, the wand would be kept wrapped in a natural fiber cloth until the Wizard needed to use it.

# MAKİNG A MAGİCAL ·WAND

T here are many contradictory traditions about which wood should be chosen for a magic wand. It is generally agreed, however, that wands made from different types of woods have different properties. One Celtic legend describes a silver-colored wand taken from a particular divine apple tree, which had the power to produce the sweetest music to lure mortals into the lands of the Gods.

Many Wizards realize that what makes a wand magical is their own intention of dedicating or consecrating the wand for magic. The modern Wizard may find the wood anywhere, ranging from his local hardware shop to the base of a tree in his favorite park. However, he should never be tempted to break a branch from a tree, since it is flaunting the laws of natural magic to take a magical tool by force.

Once the Wizard finds a piece of wood that would make an admirable wand, he will then whittle it down to a shape at one end that fits comfortably in his hand and to a length that is approximately 21 inches (53 cm).

Taking his athame (a double-edged knife — see pages 66–67), he will then carve a series of runes or other symbols to attract the power of the element of fire to strengthen his will and his ability to focus his magical power for a particular purpose. Many of the images on the wand will be symbols that relate to fire, such as an upright triangle or a dragon.

To conduct the energy through the wand, other material is sometimes incorporated with the wand. In particular, some wands are decorated with a round amethyst stone at one end, so that the energy can accumulate within the rounded stone until the Wizard is ready to aim the wand and discharge the energy.

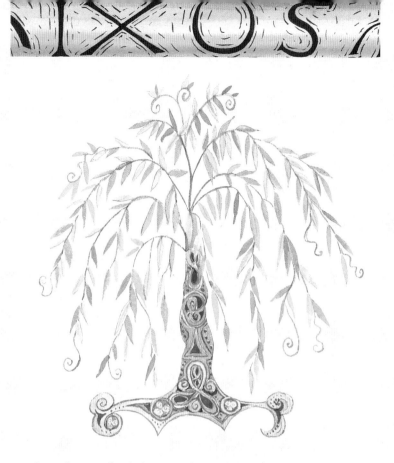

At the other end of the wand, a clear quartz crystal with a pointed edge is sometimes attached to encourage the energy to focus to a point.

In between the two stones, some Wizards wrap a decorative line of copper wire up the wand, as copper is believed to be an excellent conductor of psychic energy. In between the wire, the Wizard may write words dedicating the wand for magic or inscribe his favorite magical phrases, such as an incantation to protect him from harm when using the wand.

The Wizard will then consecrate or dedicate his new wand to the art of magic. He will empower the wand by a ritual akin to the one described on page 63, and then he will raise the wand and pledge to a higher power that the wand will only be used for magical work that will "harm none."

# OTHER POWERFUL TOOLS

Apart from the wand (see pages 62–65), a Wizard usually owns a tablet or heavy ball of metal, clay, stone, or crystal that symbolizes the element of earth. In several magical traditions, the sign of the pentagram — a five-pointed star — is inscribed on the tablet because the symbol represents the four elements and the spirit. In "white" magic the point representing the spirit must be uppermost.

The crystal ball is often used for scrying. Scrying is a form of divinatory meditation where, by focusing on a crystal ball, the blaze of the fire or the swirl of ink in a bowl of water, you will be able to see images that give you answers to your questions. The ball can also "ground" the Wizard so that when he does a powerful magical ritual he does not feel disconnected from the earth. Often magical workings require a lot of energy, and if the Wizard is not firmly "grounded" he may have trouble feeling connected with the material world.

When a Wizard wants to inscribe magical words on a candle or other object, he needs his athame, a double-edged black-handled knife, representing the element of Air and symbolizing the Wizard's intellect. The athame and the boline are both used especially for Wiccan ceremonies. The boline is a white-handled knife. The ceremonial magician would usually choose a sword.

The blades of these knives would normally be made from steel, although some magical traditions prefer to avoid metals and use other materials, such as obsidian. The athame is also used to cast a circle around the Wizard so that he is protected from any unfriendly energy forces or spirits during magical rituals.

Finally, the Wizard will need his chalice, a tool that corresponds with his emotions and the element of water. In some

occult traditions, the chalice is a tool that the Wizard must be given rather than one he or she can purchase or make. Chalices made from different materials have through the ages been associated with different magical characteristics. For instance, a chalice made from rock crystal was believed to turn cloudy if there was poison in the liquid poured into it.

### Making a Magic Carpet
### According to The Key of Solomon the King:

*Make a carpet of white and new wool, and when the Moon shall be at her full, in the Sign of Capricorn and in the hour of the Sun, thou shalt go into the country away from any habitation of man, in a place free from all impurity, and shalt spread out thy Carpet so that one of its points shall be towards the east, and another towards the west, and having made a Circle without it and enclosing it, thou shalt remain within upon the point towards the east, and holding thy wand in the air for every operation, thou shalt call upon Michael, towards the north upon RAPHAEL, towards the west upon GABRIEL, and towards the south upon URIEL.*

# POTENT POTIONS

A traditional Wizard was often approached to brew potions for various purposes. This form of low magic art was linked closely with the magical properties of various herbs. Most of the requested potions concerned the attraction of love.

Ingredients of love potions included warming spices, such as cinnamon, cloves, and even pepper, and the roots of various plants, such as ginseng and Saint John's Wort (otherwise known as John the Conqueror). One of the most potent ingredients in a love potion was the legendary satyrion root (or trifolium), mentioned in a number of ancient texts, including a story called the *Satyricon* written by the ancient Roman author Petronius.

There appears to be no modern equivalent of the satyrion, which had a bifurcated root. The lower part of the root was believed beneficial for reviving flagging interest in males and the upper part was usually used to aid women to fall pregnant. Sometimes the root of a particular orchid is labeled as satyrion root, but it is not exactly the same. If the satyrion root was dissolved in goat's milk, the potion was guaranteed to make the drinker virtually insatiable.

Mandrake was yet another root used in love potions through the ages, and was described by the ancient Greek physician Dioscorides in his *Materia Medica* as an excellent stimulant, especially when steeped in wine. Often taking the shape of a man, it came to be called Aphrodite, after the Greek Goddess of love. Dioscorides also names other ingredients for love potions, including *cardamon lepidium sativum* or cynocardamom, and even the humble turnip.

Wizards needed to take care that their potions did not have adverse side effects. If one or two ingredients that worked successfully in reviving flagging sexual interest were in fact poisonous, and the taker of the potion overdosed on the substance, the Wizard would need to learn very quickly how to avoid an angry mob.

However, not all love potions were taken internally. Some ingredients were gathered into a small bag and placed under a pillow to attract love to the person lying on it. Sometimes the ingredients would be ground up, and then blown in the face of the person whom the Wizard wished to attract or was asked for help with attracting.

# CELESTIAL TALISMANS

## WHAT ARE TALISMANS?

izards were adept at making talismans, following instructions from various sources. Many powerful talismans were outlined in one of the world's most famous grimoire, which was widely believed to have been written by King Solomon, a historical figure who had the reputation of being a master magician (see pages 10–11).

*The Key of Solomon the King* contains instructions for a number of magical procedures (see page 86), including the making of talismans. The papers that comprised the grimoire are held in the British Museum, and were translated into English by Samuel Liddell Mathers in 1888 (see pages 58–59).

There are many other sources for the design of talismans, such as Francis Barrettt's *The Magus* (1801), which contains talismanic information from earlier occult scholars such as Agrippa (see pages 18–19).

One common element in all the grimoires and magical textbooks is that a talisman is an object imbued with special powers to attract or repel certain energies. A Wizard would make a talisman to attract to its wearer protection, love, healing, or financial success.

To imbue a simple metal talisman with magical powers to help or protect its owner, the

Wizard would choose to make the talisman using a certain set of sigils or numbers, and would make the talisman on a particular day of the week to attract the right type of energy. This energy corresponds to the energy of the seven major celestial bodies identified at that time — the Sun, Moon, Mercury, Venus, Mars, Jupiter, and Saturn.

Talismanic magic is an ancient magical art and has for centuries been associated with the influence of these seven celestial bodies. Each celestial body rules the following days of the week and influences the following types of magical energy:

| Celestial body | Corresponding day of the week | Corresponding magical energy |
| --- | --- | --- |
| Sun | Sunday | Wealth, fortune, friendships |
| Moon | Monday | Diplomatic missions, reconciliation, psychic ability |
| Mercury | Wednesday | Eloquence, intelligence, business partnerships, protection against theft |
| Venus | Friday | Love, travel, friendships |
| Mars | Tuesday | Honor, courage, protection |
| Jupiter | Thursday | Acquiring riches, new friendships, preserving health |
| Saturn | Saturday | Business success, acquisition of learning, luck |

By making the talisman on a particular day and making it of a metal that corresponds to the appropriate celestial body, as well as by using the appropriate symbols, words (sometimes in Hebrew), or series of numbers, the Wizard can imbue the talisman with a delicate vibration that would magically attract the appropriate protection or help to the wearer.

The talisman does not have to be specific to one person — whoever wears it will attract the energy for which it was made. However, it is also possible to make a talisman that applies to a particular person (see page 79).

## Talisman for Love

**P**opular talismans to attract love often correspond to the energy of the planet Venus. This planet is named after the Roman Goddess of Love, and governs all spells of attraction, love potions, and other kinds of spells of the heart. To make a talisman to attract love, follow the instructions below and create the talisman with good intention and compassion.

### What do I need?
- Musk incense (optional)
- A copper disc about 2½ in (5 cm) in diameter (or a copper-colored circle of cardboard)
- A green permanent marker pen
- A sharp needle or engraver (optional)
- A piece of parchment paper or parchment-like paper (preferably 2½ in (5 cm) wide, though the precise length is not important)
- A green drawstring silk bag big enough to hold the copper disc
- A black leather thong (optional)

### When should I make this talisman?
The talisman should be made on a Friday. To calculate planetary hours, see the "Wizard's Tip" on page 77.

### What should I do?
Light the incense stick, and on one side of the copper disc draw or engrave the combination of a magic square, the divine number of the Seraphim, the "Intelligence of Venus," and the corresponding zodiac sign for Venus (see illustration right, and refer to diagram on page 146 for numbers required).

On the reverse of the copper disc, engrave or draw the sigils as accurately as possible (see right).

When you have finished inscribing the symbols for your love talisman, write the following words on a piece of parchment paper:

*Sator, Arepo, Tenet, Opera, Rotas, Iah, Iah , Iah, Enam, Iah, Iah, Iah, Kether, Chokmah, Binah, Gedulah, Geburah, Tiphereth, Netzach, Hod, Yesod, Malkuth, Abraham, Isaac, Jacob, Shadrach, Meshach, Abednego, be ye all present in my aid and for whatsoever I shall desire to obtain.*

It is very important to remember to only write this incantation if what you want accords with your true will and "it harms none." Roll up the parchment tightly and insert it, with the disc, into the green bag. Pull the drawstrings closed and either carry the talisman with you in your right-hand pocket or wear it as a pendant near your heart. To wear the talisman, tie the bag in the middle of the length of leather thong and tie the ends together so that you can wear it around your neck.

Other talismans for love have been made over the centuries. Some were in the shape of a phallus while others sported images of a bull or a dove. However, the use of the celestial influence of Venus persisted, as some talismans were merely inscribed with the astrological symbol for Venus, or simply the name "Venus" or even just a "V."

## Talisman for Protection

There are many types of talismans for various forms of protection, such as protection during your travels, protection against theft and protection against the evil eye. If you wish to have a general all-purpose protection against harm, make a talisman corresponding with Mars. Mars is the planet that relates to the warrior of the zodiac.

### What do I need?
- Basil essential oil (optional)
- Oil burner, water and tea light (optional)
- An iron disc about 2½ in (5 cm) in diameter (or a piece of cedar wood)
- A red permanent marker pen
- A sharp needle or engraver (optional)
- A red drawstring silk bag big enough to hold the disc
- A piece of parchment paper or parchment-like paper (preferably 2½ in (5 cm) wide — though the precise length is not important)
- A black leather thong (optional)

### When should I make this talisman?
The talisman should be made on a Tuesday. To calculate planetary hours, see the "Wizard's Tip" on page 77.

### What should I do?
Measure five drops of the essential oil, place in your oil burner and light the tea light. Smell the aromatic scent of basil while you draw or engrave the following combination on one side of the disc: a magic square corresponding to Mars, one of the letters of the "holy name" in Hebrew, as well as the Hebrew for the divine name of Adonai, a "good angel" that presides over Mars, Graphiel (the "Intelligence" of Mars), and Barzabel (the "Spirit of Mars"). The

talisman should also include the divine number that corresponds with Graphiel and Barzabel, and the zodiac sign that relates to Mars (see illustration left, and refer to diagram on page 146 for numbers required).

On the reverse of the disc, engrave or draw the sigils on the right as accurately as possible.

Insert the disc in the red bag. Pull the drawstrings closed and either carry the talisman with you in your right-hand pocket or wear it as a pendant near your heart.

(refer to diagram on page 146 for numbers required)

## WIZARD'S TIP

*Once a talisman has been made using the appropriate materials, and burning the appropriate incense and performing the task on the right day and at the right time, some Wizards also "charge" it by saying out loud what its purpose will be.*

*A number of grimoires have a set phrase that can be incanted or written down. However, if you speak from the heart about the purpose for which you have dedicated the talisman, this will usually be effective enough to "charge" the object with your magical intent. Here is an example of the type of phrase you may wish to adopt or adapt to charge your talisman:*

*"I call upon my symbol of [protection (love) (success) (healing), etc] the power of earth, air, fire, and water, blessing this talisman with purity of purpose and protecting it from influences of harm, known and unknown."*

## Talisman for Success

The brilliance and glow of the Sun can attract fame, popularity and fortune to the wearer of a talisman that corresponds with its energy. Collect the following ingredients and perform the instructions as closely as possible.

### What do I need?
- Frankincense or myrrh incense
- A gold-colored disc about 2½ in (5 cm) in diameter (or a piece of yellow cardboard)
- A black permanent marker pen
- A sharp needle or engraver (optional)
- A gold drawstring silk bag big enough to hold the gold-colored disc
- A black leather thong (optional)

### When should I make this talisman?
The talisman should be made on a Sunday. To calculate planetary hours, see the "Wizard's Tip" on the opposite page.

### What should I do?
Light the incense stick, and on one side of the disc, draw or engrave the combination of a magic square, the zodiac sign for the Sun and the Hebrew letters for the "holy name" (see illustration right, and refer to diagram on page 146 for numbers required), as well as for Nachiel (the "Intelligence of the Sun") and Sorath (the "Spirit of the Sun"). The talisman should also include the divine number for Sorath.

On the reverse of the disc, engrave or draw the sigils on the left as accurately as possible.

Insert the disc in the gold bag. Pull the drawstrings closed and either carry the talisman with you in your right-hand pocket or wear it as a pendant. To wear the talisman, tie the bag in the middle of the length of leather thong and tie the ends together so that you can wear it around your neck.

## Wizard's tip

*Some Wizards are keen to make a certain talisman not only on a particular day, but also at a particular time of the day or night. Below is a table of the planetary hours of the day.*

| | Sunday | Monday | Tuesday | Wednesday | Thursday | Friday | Saturday |
|---|---|---|---|---|---|---|---|
| 1 | Sun | Moon | Mars | Mercury | Jupiter | Venus | Saturn |
| 2 | Venus | Saturn | Sun | Moon | Mars | Mercury | Jupiter |
| 3 | Mercury | Jupiter | Venus | Saturn | Sun | Moon | Mars |
| 4 | Moon | Mars | Mercury | Jupiter | Venus | Saturn | Sun |
| 5 | Saturn | Sun | Moon | Mars | Mercury | Jupiter | Venus |
| 6 | Jupiter | Venus | Saturn | Sun | Moon | Mars | Mercury |
| 7 | Mars | Mercury | Jupiter | Venus | Saturn | Sun | Moon |
| 8 | Sun | Moon | Mars | Mercury | Jupiter | Venus | Saturn |
| 9 | Venus | Saturn | Sun | Moon | Mars | Mercury | Jupiter |
| 10 | Mercury | Jupiter | Venus | Saturn | Sun | Moon | Mars |
| 11 | Moon | Mars | Mercury | Jupiter | Venus | Saturn | Sun |
| 12 | Saturn | Sun | Moon | Mars | Mercury | Jupiter | Venus |

*To calculate the planetary hour of the day, you will need to start counting from the exact time of sunrise. To calculate the planetary hour of the night, start counting from sunset. You will also find that according to the Season, the length of day and night varies, and this affects the length of each planetary "hour."*

*On the day before you wish to make your spell, note the time of the sunrise and the time of the sunset. Calculate the minutes between sunrise and sunset, and then divide the number of minutes into twelve. This will be the length of the planetary "hour" at the time you are making the talisman. Use this unit of time to calculate the correct time to make the talisman. All the talismans that you will be making according to the instructions in this book should be constructed during the daytime. Talismans that should be constructed during the night are those that have a secret or destructive purpose, and should never be considered lightly.*

## Talisman for Healing

**M**any healing talismans vibrate with the planet Jupiter. Jupiter is connected not only to healing but also to acquiring fortunes and quenching desires, and can be used for a talisman to attract wealth and material possessions. Collect the following implements and follow the instructions as closely as you can.

### What do I need?
- A stick of pine incense (optional)
- A tin disc about 2½ in (5 cm) in diameter (or a circle this size made out of silver-colored cardboard)
- A blue permanent marker pen
- A sharp needle or engraver (optional)
- A blue drawstring silk bag big enough to hold the disc
- A black leather thong (optional)

### When should I make this talisman?
The talisman should be made on a Thursday. To calculate planetary hours, see the "Wizard's Tip" on page 77.

### What should I do?
Light the incense stick, and on one side of the disc, engrave or draw the combination of a magic square, and Hebrew symbols corresponding to Jupiter (see illustration left, and refer to the diagram on page 146 for numbers required).

On the reverse of the disc, draw or engrave the sigils on the right as accurately as possible.

Insert the disc into the blue bag. Pull the drawstrings closed, and either carry the talisman with you in your right-hand pocket or wear it as a pendant. To wear the talisman, tie the bag in the middle of the length of leather thong and tie the ends together. For amulets that protect against illness, see pages 80–83.

If you would like to make this healing talisman for a particular person who is unwell, ask that person's permission before making the talisman. If you are given permission, personalize the talisman as outlined in the Wizard's Tip below.

## Wizard's Tip

### *Making the spell specific for a particular person*

*To do this, you will need to translate the letters of your name or your friend's name into numbers. There are many ways of doing this — try the following simple system. Each number corresponds to a set of letters. If your name has an "A" in it, this letter corresponds with a 1. If your name has an "N" in it, this letter corresponds to 5. Work out the rest of the letters of your name.*

| 1 | 2 | 3 | 4 | 5 | 6 | 7 | 8 | 9 |
|---|---|---|---|---|---|---|---|---|
| A | B | C | D | E | F | G | H | I |
| J | K | L | M | N | O | P | Q | R |
| S | T | U | V | W | X | Y | Z |   |

*For example, if you are making a healing spell for a person called "Anton," you will pick out the following numbers on the magic square. To signify the beginning of the name, draw a small circle over the number before drawing a line to the next letter of the name. To end the name, draw a short perpendicular line over the number corresponding with the last letter of the person's name.*

| 4 | 14 | 15 | 1 |
|---|---|---|---|
| 9 | 7 | 6 | 12 |
| 5 | 11 | 10 | 8 |
| 16 | 2 | 3 | 13 |

*This will condense the power of your friend's name into a powerful symbol, which can be used, with that person's permission, for his or her benefit for a future magic spell.*

# PROTECTIVE AMULETS

## WHAT ARE AMULETS?

There are several types of amulets, but all types are usually used to evoke magical protection. In ancient Egypt, amulets were made to protect against a myriad of inconveniences and disasters. These protective amulets were called either *sa* or *mkt*. Another form of amulet also evolved: one that could bestow useful attributes, such as health. In Egypt, these were called *wedja*.

Other cultures also commonly used amulets. One of the main types of protective amulet, which was mentioned by the Roman philosopher Pliny the Elder, is those used as a protection against illness.

A homeopathic approach was taken with this kind of amulet, which would usually contain the very substance that had caused the illness. Poison or other substances would be included, often in powdered form, in a box or bottle that would be worn against the person's skin. If the amulet were to protect the person's heart or other organ, the appropriate amulet would be worn near that particular area of the body.

Amulets also worked on the basis of "like attracts like." An amulet in the shape of a heart was used to protect the heart from physical irregularities, as well as from suffering heartbreak over a lover or friend.

Amulets were also used for personal protection. This type included amulets in the form of religious designs, such as the Egyptian ankh, the Christian Cross and the Jewish Star of David. These designs are symbols of a divine power that will

protect the faithful. For Wizards, the pentagram is a powerful religious design. With its single point rising upward, the pentagram is symbolic of the harmonious balance of the four elements and the spirit, which protects and promotes life.

The Jewish Star of David, a six-pointed star, was also used as a powerful protection against evil and enchantment from a rival Wizard. The six-pointed star comprises two triangles, one pointing upward and the other downward. This was the main component of the famous "Seal of Solomon," believed to be the ultimate

The Jewish Star of David.

amulet of protection for a Wizard. It is representative of the highest universal law of the balance of opposites, of the balance between the macrocosm that is the Cosmos and the microcosm that is a human being. It is also accompanies the saying:

*As Above, So Below.*

Natural objects were also valued for their magical powers. Animals' claws were believed to give hunters an advantage in hunting particular animals without being killed by them; also, carrying the feather of a bird, for example a hawk, would imbue the wearer with the gifts of the creature. In the case of the hawk, this gift could be keen sight.

Amulets made from natural objects, such as stones, gems or shells, all have certain energies that protect the wearer from particular threats or attract certain forms of energy. For example, a citrine (a yellow quartz crystal) may be worn to protect the wearer from nightmares and to enhance his or her psychic abilities.

## How to Make an Amulet

Amulets were often used in necklaces to provide permanent protection against unfriendly supernatural forces and the major fears of life – death, poverty, and ill health. Collect the listed ingredients to make the following "all-purpose" amulet in the form of a bag that can be worn around the neck.

**What do I need?**
- A piece of red agate
- A piece of lapis lazuli
- A pinch of dried sage
- A silver or silver-colored ankh
- A piece of parchment paper or parchment like paper (preferably 2½ inches (5 cm) wide — though the precise length is not important)
- A black marker pen
- A length of red string or ribbon (to bind around the piece of paper once it is rolled into a tight scroll)
- A red drawstring silk bag big enough to hold the above ingredients
- A black leather thong

**When should I make this talisman?**
During the New Moon.

**What should I do?**
Place the first four ingredients in the bag. The agate is included to symbolize longevity. It can also be used as an amulet on its own to purify the blood and to soothe fevers, the lapis lazuli aids in psychic protection. Sage is renowned for its association with longevity, and the Egyptian ankh is included as an ancient symbol of life.

Write the following words on the piece of paper:
*Life, Prosperity, Health*

These three words were written in hieroglyphics on the back of many ancient Egyptian amulets. Many believed that the corresponding hieroglyphics themselves were inherently magical.

Roll the paper into a tight scroll, and tie the red string or ribbon to secure it. Place it in the bag with the other ingredients. Pull the drawstrings closed and tie the leather thong around the bag where convenient. Tie the ends of the thong, and hang this powerful amulet around your neck. In Egyptian magic many amulets were worn around the neck, as this area was seen as vulnerable to weaknesses, such as the risk of choking to death.

## Wizard's Tip

*Sometimes the words "amulet" and "talisman" are used interchangeably, although strictly speaking "amulet" means a protective magical object while "talisman" is an object that has a magical charge, which can either protect against certain events or enhance particular occult energies.*

*Eliphas Lévi, in* The History of Magic, *discussed the making of the "talisman of talismans" – King Solomon's Ring. A ring usually has amuletic properties; however, the Ring of Solomon is a particularly special one:*

*"The Ring of Solomon is at once round and square and it represents the mystery of the quadrature of the circle. It is composed of seven squares so arranged that they form a circle. Their bezels are sound and square, one being of gold and the other of silver. The Ring should be a filagree of the seven metals. In the silver setting a white stone is placed and in the gold one there is a red stone. The white stone bears the sign of the Macrocosm, while the Microcosm is on the red stone. When the Ring is worn upon the finger, one of the stones should be turned inward and the other outward ..."*

# mAGICAL GRIMOIRES

## WHAT IS A GRIMOIRE?

Over the centuries, a great number of books have claimed to hold the secret of making substances with legendary powers, such as the Elixir of Life, or the Philosopher's Stone, with its ability to heal any disease and transmute base metals into gold. Some Wizards have been exceedingly fond of studying these texts, called grimoires, in order to attain secret knowledge and power over supernatural forces.

A grimoire is a book of magic that contains spells, rituals, incantations and instructions on how to perform certain magical procedures, such as making yourself invisible, being in two places at the same time, or even making a magic carpet. Grimoires are said to date back to the thirteenth century and are believed to have been written since the time of King Solomon.

After the 1500s the flourishing of interest in the occult led to the printing of grimoires, which by the nineteenth century came to be translated into English. Samuel Liddell MacGregor Mathers translated into English one of the most celebrated of grimoires, *The Key of Solomon the King*, in 1888.

Hierarchies of spirits, of angels, and of intelligences, and their connection with corresponding celestial energies are often a substantial topic of discussion in the grimoires. Francis Barrett, in his 1801 publication *The Magus*, went one step further and included color drawings supposedly showing what some of these entities looked like. The fearsome pictures were an excellent deterrent to anyone tempted to call these spirits forth.

The names of these supernatural entities, often in Hebrew, were sometimes divulged. The knowledge of an entity's name was one way of connecting with it and attracting its power. A number of the grimoires purported to give the secret true name of God and gave instructions on how to use it respectfully and with great effect.

Over the centuries, stories have been told of uninitiated people unwittingly uttering a spell from a grimoire or a Wizard's special book of spells and coming to a sticky end because they called up more than they could handle. The legend of the Sorcerer's Apprentice is an excellent cautionary tale about the negative results of exercising powers that you have no experience in handling.

Another story involves the unfortunate end of a student who bribed a housekeeper to allow him to see the spell book of Henry Cornelius Agrippa von Nettesheim (see pages 18–19) while he was living in Louvain. Agrippa was away for the day, so the young man, blazing with curiosity, persuaded the housekeeper to let him into Agrippa's study to read the book of spells. While he was reading the book, the student raised a very angry spirit, who took his life.

In Barrett's *The Magus*, the story continues that upon Agrippa's return to the house, he saw spirits dancing on his rooftop and found the dead body in the study. With his magical knowledge, Agrippa managed to reanimate the dead body by commanding one of the spirits to possess the flesh and make it walk down the stairs into the marketplace. Agrippa hoped that by making the body move away from his residence he would not be held responsible for the young man's death. This was a forlorn hope, as the young man's death was still considered suspicious, and Agrippa was hounded out of the town. According to Barrett, Agrippa's *Books of Magic* (*De Occulta Philosophia*) were translated into English and published in London in 1651.

# THE KEY OF SOLOMON THE KING
## (CLAVICULA SALOMONIS)

King Solomon is reputed to have been the legendary author of this grimoire (see pages 10–11). The grimoire's fame comes predominantly from the fact that it contains instructions on how to summon various spirits and get them to do the summoner's bidding. In another text, *The Testament of Solomon*, the story is told of how the King derives his power over the spirits or demons from a ring given to him by an angel sent from God. Other spells of notoriety in this grimoire included those that were specifically designed to bring death and destruction to another person.

Although some of the spells were manipulative and destructive, the importance of the work is still immeasureable. Samuel Liddell MacGregor Mathers proclaimed that the grimoire was "the fountain-head and storehouse of Qabalistical Magic [see pages 118–119], and the origin of much of the Ceremonial Magic [see pages 120–121] of mediaeval times."

There are numerous versions of the *Key of Solomon*. The English translation by Mathers attempts to marry several versions that are held at the British Museum, including a late sixteenth-century version. In his translation, Mathers was careful to exclude those spells that could be classified as "black magic," warning that those who determine "to work evil, be assured that that evil will recoil on himself and that he will be struck by the reflex current."

# BOOK OF SHADOWS

The first reference to a *Book of Shadows* came from Gerald Gardner (see pages 32–33). He included in his own Book all manner of rituals, spells and other magical notes and procedures when evolving a magical movement that would come to be known as Wicca.

Gardner at first collated his *Book of Shadows* from a number of sources, including Aleister Crowley (see pages 30–31) and Charles Leland's *Aradia: The Gospel of the Witches*. However, Gardner and his working partner in magic, Doreen Valiente, revised and rewrote subsequent versions of the *Book of Shadows*.

Valiente has noted that in 1949 Gardner came upon the idea of calling a book of "rituals and magical information" a *Book of Shadows*, and has speculated that the name may have came from a Sanskrit manuscript about divination achieved by measuring the length of a person's shadow.

This workbook of information and rituals was passed down from Witch or Wizard to each newly initiated member of a coven or smaller group. It was often a condition of initiation that the initiate should copy out the initiator's *Book of Shadows*. Gardner himself urged that the initiate, when copying a ritual or spell, should include his or her own additions.

During the decades since Gardner first called his magical notes a *Book of Shadows*, nearly every Witch and Wizard has referred to his or her own book or journal of effective spells and rituals as a *Book of Shadows*. Not only does this book contains spells and rituals that the Witch or Wizard has copied, adapted or invented, but it is also a useful tool as a journal for jotting down feelings, visions and insights garnered during a magical ritual.

# STARTING YOUR OWN WIZARD'S JOURNAL

Consider starting your own Wizard's journal to keep in one place all your ideas and information about spells, seasonal celebrations and other short rituals you are interested in using. The journal can be anything from an ordinary exercise book to a special journal made by hand from recycled or rice paper.

You may even consider using a ring binder so that when you have more information on a particular type of magic you can simply add an extra page in the appropriate place to keep all the spells of a similar category in the one place. It is best that the book can be locked or kept in a specially made bag so that no one can look at your magical work unless you wish it.

Your Wizard's journal is a very private book. In it you will keep not only information about the type of magic that appeals to you, but also lists of what you want in life and strategies of how to achieve this in both the magical and material worlds.

You can also include information about the results of your spells, taking particular note of any vivid dreams that you may have the night after a spell. Keep your journal beside your bed and as soon as you wake up write down any dreams that you can remember.

Dreams are particularly useful for giving you insight about your life and your magical work. Examining your dreams after performing spells and other magical work can also help strengthen your intuition. The best way to improve your intuitive powers is to take notice of your dreams and feelings.

When writing down a special spell that you would like to try, leave a couple of pages so you can note exactly how you

performed the spell. Put in as many details as possible of what you were feeling when preparing and doing the spell, what your ingredients were and how you prepared them, when you did the spell, and whether you noticed any particularly unusual or curious events after the spell was cast or the magical ritual was performed.

This is invaluable information about your own personal powers of magic. Very much like a professional cook, a Wizard usually develops an expertise in a particular type of magic, favoring a certain range of ingredients and substances that he feels work well for him.

## Wizard's Tip

*To keep your journal safe from prying eyes, place a black feather inside the pages as an amulet of protection.*

# CHAPTER 4
# WIZARDLY MYSTERIES

## INTRODUCTION: A WELL-ROUNDED EDUCATION

A Wizard often has a scholarly interest in a wide range of topics. He can be equally well versed in the sciences and the arts. A Wizard can be adept at alchemy (see pages 92–95) as well as understanding the psychological imperatives of the people seeking his magical expertise (see pages 100–102).

Alchemy was an art, the origins of which seemed to have been lost in the mists of time. Various historical and mythical characters have at one time or another been thought to have brought alchemy into being — for example, Isis, an important Egyptian Goddess, Hermes Trismegistus, an Egyptian priest who became the patron of alchemy and other sacred procedures, and King Solomon.

Magic was particularly popular in the eighteenth century, when a number of secret societies flourished and the translations of old grimoires were popular. During this time there was also a great interest in the rational mind, the ability of the mind to solve problems, and the use of the mind to effect change. Magic came to be valued as an important, ritualized way of helping the mind to focus upon achieving a certain results in life. Riddles were useful in helping the Wizard use his mind without prejudice and free from presumption (see page 103).

Wizards have often been trained to be able to perceive clearly both the "big picture" (or macrocosm) and the details that can help magic happen (or microcosm). Many Wizards have found solace in thinking about the Cosmos as an ordered system. One of the most influential systems that explained the flow of occult energy through the world and the Cosmos is the Kabbalah (see pages 118–119). Many rituals of Ceremonial Magic (see pages 120–121) are based on the Kabbalah.

A Wizard understood that insight into the mysteries of everyday life stemmed from observing the Cosmos, and that the movement of the planets can affect many aspects of the everyday. This knowledge aided him in tapping into the future. Many Wizards have learned astrology (see pages 104–107) and used the Tarot (see pages 108–111), which are cards based in part on the four elements and on images that represent the various stages of life. Mathematics and numerology were also a powerful form of magic, where individual numbers had hidden occult qualities that a Wizard had to learn (see pages 116–117).

Having such information at hand often led a Wizard to wonder how to control completely and transcend his immediate environment. Spells abounded, instructing the Wizard on how to fly (see page 114), become invisible (see page 113) and control the weather (see page 115).

Sometimes the things a Wizard seeks to achieve require more power than he can possibly summon, so the Wizard will invoke the help of supernatural entities, in the shape of angels and spirits (see pages 122–123) or friendly, spiritually attuned animals called familiars or power animals (see pages 124–125).

Through the ages, it has been believed that knowledge of the occult has the ability to perfect the mind and bring the Wizard closer to divinity.

# ALCHEMY

## GOLD

Gold was one of the most precious metals used in magic. Believed to be the most direct link to the highest divine power, gold has been sought over the centuries by Wizards for use in their spells and other magical work. Some Wizards have incorporated a sliver of gold into their wands to encourage success in their magic.

Gold is associated with the Sun, and has been used for spells designed to attract riches, respect and honor. Talismans made for this purpose were often made from golden discs. In Francis Barrett's *The Magus* (1801), there is reference to a talismanic disc or plate being made out of pure gold.

Pure gold cannot be manipulated into an object, as it is too soft. Since ancient times, gold (as well as silver) has been fashioned into jewellery and other objects when mixed with alloys (such as copper), which have been inscribed with the appropriate symbols (see page 76) corresponding to the energy of the Sun.

Alchemists, whose numbers included many Wizards, often sought ways of creating gold from base metals. This was the legend behind the "Philosopher's Stone" and its ability to create gold of the finest quality. As many Wizards were scholars and often at the beck and call of wealthy patrons, the promise of independent wealth lured them to search for this magical treasure that would liberate them from a life of servitude or poverty (see pages 96–97).

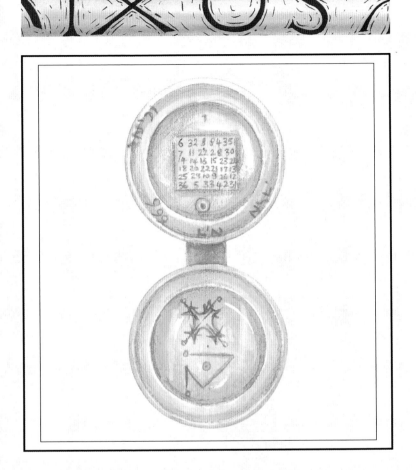

*From Francis Barrett's* The Magus *(1801):*
"... *Sol [the Sun] being fortunate, renders him that wears
[its symbols] renowned, amiable, acceptable, potent in all his
works, and equals him to a king, elevating his fortunes, and
enabling him to do whatever he will.*"

## Silver

A number of alchemists believed in the occult saying "As Above, So Below," which meant for both alchemists and Wizards that the metals coming from the earth or "made" by the processes of alchemy were linked to the energies of the celestial bodies.

Silver was used for talismans associated with the Moon, which, according to Francis Barrett in *The Magus*, make:

> *... the bearer amiable, pleasant, cheerful, and honoured, removing all malice and ill-will; it causes security in a journey, increase of riches, and health of body; drives away enemies ...*

Silver, symbolizing the light of the Moon, was often associated with the Goddess, and gold symbolized sunlight and the divine masculine energy of the God. Silver was used in magical rituals as a metal to encourage a harmonious energy and a sense of peace. The chalice (see page 67), which in ritual magic corresponds to female/Goddess energy, is often made of silver, and features in celebrations held during new or full moon.

### Wizard's Tip

*The following metals were believed to correspond to the energies of the following celestial bodies. However, there were some disagreements between grimoires. Francis Barrett offered some alternative suggestions in* The Magus.

| Celestial bodies | Corresponding metals | Corresponding substances according to Barrett (1801) |
|---|---|---|
| Sun | Gold | Gold |
| Moon | Silver | Silver |
| Mercury | Mercury | Silver, tin, yellow brass or virgin parchment |
| Venus | Copper | Silver |
| Mars | Iron | Iron |
| Jupiter | Tin | Silver |
| Saturn | Lead | Lead |

## Copper

Copper corresponds to the energy of Venus, the Goddess of love, and has been used to decorate a number of occult tools because of its ability to conduct psychic energy as well as heat and electricity.

As copper is also believed to have associations with the element of Earth, a dish or plaque made from this metal is placed by some Wizards under their crystal ball (a symbol of the Earth element – see page 66) to help stabilize its energy.

Copper has energies of both attraction and protection. Place a copper coin in your purse or wallet to attract more money to you. Wear a copper ring whenever you expect to be in a situation of confrontation or if you want to attract love.

Of course, copper also has strong healing properties, with many believing that wearing copper over a particular joint will alleviate the symptoms of arthritis. It also is believed to have the ability to ease cramps and, if worn near the liver, to help a traveler overcome motion sickness.

### Wizard's Quote

*From Francis Barrett's* The Magus *(1801):*

*"… Venus being fortunate, promotes concord, ends strife, procures the love of women, helps conception, is good against barrenness, gives ability for generation, dissolves enchantments, causes peace between man and woman, … it likewise drives away melancholy [and] distempers, and causes joyfulness; and this carried about travelers makes them fortunate."*

*Caution: Francis Barrett advocated that a love talisman should be made from silver, rather than copper, and instructed that, when making a silver talisman for love corresponding with Venus, it should be ensured that the silver is not alloyed with brass, as brass causes the contrary indications.*

# THE PHILOSOPHER'S STONE

The ultimate goal of any alchemist was to make the Philosopher's Stone. It was searched for and allegedly found at Glastonbury in England by Dr John Dee and Edward Kelly (see pages 22–23) as a bottle of elixir. Many stories have also been told of mysterious individuals approaching alchemists and selling them, at exorbitant prices, a small segment of the Philosopher's Stone.

One such incident befell Helvetius, otherwise known as John Frederick Schweitzer, the famous Dutch physician to William of Orange. In 1666, a stranger approached Helvetius with three pieces of transparent crystals with a sulfurous glow and the claim that the crystals were the Philosopher's Stone and had the ability to heal, promote longevity and transmute base metals into gold.

Four alchemical stages, called "The Head of the Crow and the Red Lion," in the production of the Philosopher's Stone. From J D Mylius, *Anatomia Auri*, 1628.

Eventually, Helvetius was able to create an iridescent substance that changed from hues of bright green to blood red during the cooling process. He claimed that when the preparation had finally cooled he discovered that he had made pure gold.

The power of the Philosopher's Stone was legendary. Various grimoires and magical texts gave instructions on the making of this substance. Francis Barrett, in *The Magus* (1801), preferred the instructions on making the stone given by the Belgian physician Jan Baptista van Helmont, who is now considered a pioneer in medicine and chemistry.

Helmont described the stone as being the color of saffron, shining with the appearance of "bruised" glass, and able to make eight ounces (240 g) of "the most pure gold" from the "fourth part of one grain."

Barrett also put together a list of "lessons" that would qualify a person for the search of the Philosopher's Stone. These include the following instructions:

- Cast away any "vile affections," deceit, hypocrisy, profligacy and profane speaking.
- Keep your own and your neighbor's secrets. Do not despise the poor and do not pander to the rich.
- Give to the needy and the unfortunate.
- Be merciful to those who offend you.
- Do not be hasty to condemn and despise scandal and "tattling." Let your words be few.
- Do not succumb to drunkenness.
- Avoid gluttony and all excess.
- Do not covet much gold, and learn to be satisfied with enough.

Barrett strongly warned his readers against being tempted to obtain the Philosopher's Stone from an individual who professed to have the secret of how to make it. Even in 1801 there were a number of people in London who claimed to have the stone, tempting the credulous to purchase it at an enormous price.

# THE ELEMENTS

The elements are the building blocks of not only the world and all living creatures and vegetation, but also of magical procedures. Each element – Earth, Air, Fire, and Water – had a corresponding meaning in terms of the soul, psychology and physiology of human beings (see pages 100–101), as well as occult

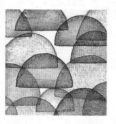

relationships with various supernatural entities, such as angels, devils, "intelligences" and even the Supreme Being.

It was believed that everything around and within us is a certain mixture or union of various elements that have the ability to change into each other, as hardened earth can turn into watery mud when enough moisture is introduced. The elements are also a study of opposites. Fire and Air are considered light substances, whereas Earth and Water are heavy.

Plato considered that Fire was bright, thin and active while Earth was dark, thick and passive. Air had some qualities of Fire and less of Earth, and was believed to be thin, dark and active while Water had more qualities of Earth than Fire, and was considered dark, thick and active.

It was believed that without the knowledge of these elements a Wizard could not be, according to Francis Barrett in *The Magus* (1801), "confident that he can work any thing in the Occult Sciences of Magic and Nature."

In ceremonial magic and other rituals of magic, the four elements were invoked. They were invoked into the magical working in a number of ways. Those interested in working with

angels (see pages 122–123) personified the elements as the four archangels.

In other magical workings, the elements are considered forms of energy that can be tapped into for a particular type of spell or other magical procedure. Each element also corresponds with one of the main compass directions — north, south, east, and west. Each magical tradition has its own correspondences, but it is most commonly believed that you can invoke the element of:

• Earth facing north (south in the southern hemisphere);
• Air facing east (west in the southern hemisphere);
• Fire facing south (north in the southern hemisphere);
• Water facing west (east in the southern hemisphere).

The element may be further "asked" to aid in certain types of magical workings. Earth is often invoked for spells to attract money for a particular project, financial comfort, and fertility. Air is invoked for magical workings to do with spiritual development, to strengthen the intuition,  and to aid in examinations. Fire is useful in purifying negative energies, and for giving extra power to a spell. Water is particularly invoked for spells concerning the heart and the emotions.

## WIZARD'S TIP

*The following archangels can be invoked for the following elements:*
*• Earth – Uriel • Air – Raphael*
*• Fire – Michael • Water – Gabriel*

# PSYCHOLOGY

## THE FOUR HUMORS

Since medieval times, attempts have been made to link people's appearance to their behavior, giving the Wizard and the physician a system for understanding how physical illnesses can affect different types of people and the nature of the associated illnesses and mental states.

Since ancient times, people have been viewed as having one of a certain number of body types. In the West, these were classified as melancholic, phlegmatic, choleric and sanguine. Many ancient civilizations had their own ways of systematizing the different body types.

In India, Ayurvedic practitioners divided human beings into the kapha, pitta and vata body types. Kapha types were often heavy set, with a dark, oily complexion and a stable, measured way of thinking. Pitta types were of medium build with fair, easily blemished skin, and when out of balance tended toward anger. Vata types were lean and of slim build, with dry skin and were usually quick witted, but easily tired.

In the West and in Ayurvedic medicine, each body type was linked to a particular element or combination of elements. In the West, the following links were made:

| Western body types | Associated elements | Associated personalities | Associated zodiac signs |
|---|---|---|---|
| Choleric | Fire | Aggressive and imaginative | Leo |
| Sanguine | Air | Intellectual and easily bored | Aquarius |
| Melancholic | Earth | Reliable and sensible | Taurus |
| Phlegmatic | Water | Sensitive and inward looking | Scorpio |

In India, there is a belief that the world and everything in it is composed of five elements — Ether or spirit, as well as Earth, Air, Fire, and Water. The combination of two elements are believed to create the following body types:

| Associated elements | Ayurvedic body types |
|---|---|
| Ether and Air | Vata |
| Fire and Water | Pitta |
| Earth and Water | Kapha |

Interestingly, Ether (called Akasa) was also acknowledged in Western occultism, particularly in the study of the Kabbalah.

When devising a magical solution for a person, a Wizard would take into account the person's disposition. To strengthen the client's purpose or resolve, the Wizard may include ingredients in the spell that correspond to or enhance the client's ruling element. For instance, if the client is a choleric type seeking to improve his or her creative powers, the Wizard could include in the spell items that resonate with the element of Fire, such as garlic, amber, or brass.

However, if the person is too aggressive and needs a spell to help him or her feel more settled, the Wizard would include ingredients in the spell that help stabilize Fire, such as those that resonate with the element of Air — for example, star anise, aventurine, or tin. It is important to remember that the elements of Fire and Air blend well together, as do Earth and Water.

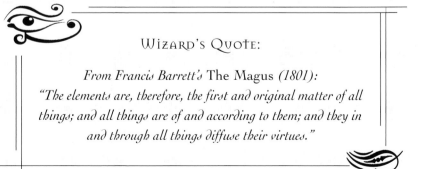

WIZARD'S QUOTE:

From Francis Barrett's The Magus (1801):
"The elements are, therefore, the first and original matter of all things; and all things are of and according to them; and they in and through all things diffuse their virtues."

## Understanding Wishes

To create an effective spell, a specific situation or specific type of person, the Wizard should have knowledge of a wide range of topics and a strong sense of intuition.

This intuition will also aid the Wizard in determining what a person is really asking for. If a Wizard is asked to provide a spell to attract wealth, he needs to work out whether the person is really asking for money to buy his or her own home, or to pay for a child's schooling. Often the person making the request is not sure what he or she wants.

Intuition is a powerful tool, and if you are an aspiring Wizard or Witch, it can be strengthened by observation and by taking notice of your feelings, thoughts and dreams. See pages 88–89 about starting your own Wizard's journal or *Book of Shadows* to catch your insights before, during and after doing any magical work, such as casting spells or making talismans.

Intuition is often linked with the phases of the Moon. Traditionally, a Wizard's intuition is strongest at full moon or at new moon. By wearing a stone or metal that resonates with the Moon, a Wizard ensures that he will be able to tap into this ability whenever he wants. Here is a list of objects that can be worn to help enhance intuition.

**Objects that can be worn or carried to enhance intuition**
- A silver disc
- A silver pendant in the shape of a pentagram
- A moonstone pendant or ring in a silver setting
- A white cloth bag containing a star anise, nine dried petals of a white rose, and a pinch of ginger

## Riddles and clear thinking

Riddles occurred in myths and legends to challenge the clear mindedness of a Wizard or hero on a quest. A "threshold guardian," an entity that barred passage, often asked the riddle to test the worthiness of an adventurer.

One of the most famous riddles is found in Greek mythology, posed by a Sphinx that perched outside the city of Thebes, killing all those who could not answer. Finally Oedipus answered the question correctly and was made King of Thebes. The Sphinx fell off its perch and died.

In Egypt, there was a belief that the deceased needed help in crossing into *Neter-Khert* (the afterworld). Papyrus scrolls were placed beside mummies in their coffins so that the deceased had a reference guide to help them navigate their journey safely into *Neter-Khert*. The Egyptian dead needed their reference guides if they were to meet safely the various challenges they had to face.

When coming up against an obstacle to his learning, the wise Wizard will focus on the obstacle to understand what he needs to learn so that he can continue on his journey. Obstacles can be very useful in helping the wise strengthen their mind and their will.

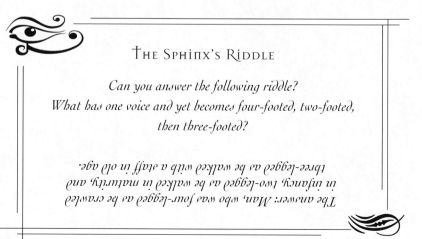

### The Sphinx's Riddle

*Can you answer the following riddle?*
*What has one voice and yet becomes four-footed, two-footed,*
*then three-footed?*

*The answer: Man, who was four-legged as he crawled in infancy, two-legged as he walked in maturity and three-legged as he walked with a staff in old age.*

# DIVINATION

## ASTROLOGY

Astrology is one of the oldest forms of divination known. It evolved into a precise system in about 3000 BC. Virtually all ancient civilizations, including the Egyptians, the Greeks, the Chinese, and the astrologers of India, have developed their own form of astrology. Astrology is based on the concept that the formation of your fate, personality, and even physical makeup is affected by the position of the Sun, Moon and planets around the earth at the time of your birth. The Greeks devised a system of twelve personality types based on this system.

| Astrological house | Summary of its aspects |
|---|---|
| First | Who you are |
| Second | Your financial leanings |
| Third | Your education |
| Fourth | Your issues at home |
| Fifth | Your creative pursuits |
| Sixth | Your career |
| Seventh | Your close relationships |
| Eighth | The cycles in your life |
| Ninth | Travels, both internally and externally |
| Tenth | Your ambitions |
| Eleventh | Your social life |
| Twelfth | The unconscious realm |

An astrologer, upon learning the time, day and year of your birth, will be able to plot the position of the planets on a chart, and work out your personality and other information about your life. The astrologer's chart comprises a circle subdivided into twelve segments, called houses. There are two primary systems, one called the "Equal House" and the other the "Placidus," by which an astrologer can work out to how to subdivide the circle accurately to represent the twelve houses. These houses correspond to the twelve aspects of life shown on page 104.

The study of astrology is an engrossing and fascinating one, requiring a great deal of commitment. Wise Wizards use astrology as a very comprehensive way of understanding people and their potential.

## HOW TO USE ASTROLOGY IN MAGIC

The study of astrology is very rewarding. It enables you not only to understand yourself and those around you, but also to work out the most auspicious time to make a talisman or to perform a particular magical ritual. Here is a list of types of magical work that correspond to the movement of the Sun through the Zodiac.

| Zodiac | Symbol | Period | Type of magic |
|---|---|---|---|
| Aries | ♈ | March 20 – April 20 | Spells for acquiring strength, cleansing anger, and protection |
| Taurus | ♉ | April 21 – May 21 | Spells for attracting love, harmony, and sexual pleasure |
| Gemini | ♊ | May 22 – June 21 | Spells for enhancing eloquence, improving negotiation skills, and gaining success in business |
| Cancer | ♋ | June 22 – July 22 | Magical work for spiritual development, for enhancing intuition and psychic connections, and spells for fertility |
| Leo | ♌ | July 23 – August 23 | Success in spells generally, spells for promotion and acknowledgment, and for gaining honor and riches |
| Virgo | ♍ | August 24 – September 23 | Spells dealing with improvement in communications, for gaining insight, and enhancing creativity |
| Libra | ♎ | September 24 – October 23 | Spells to attract friendships and love, and enhance harmony |
| Scorpio | ♏ | October 24 – November 23 | Spells for the reconciliation of differences, and protection spells against struggle and conflict |
| Sagittarius | ♐ | November 24 – December 21 | Spells for success in business, the acquisition of material possessions, and achieving acclaim |
| Capricorn | ♑ | December 22 – January 20 | Spells dealing with obstacles and limitations, and success in building projects |
| Aquarius | ♒ | January 21 – February 18 | Spells to enhance individuality and magical work affecting long-term projects |
| Pisces | ♓ | February 19 – March 19 | Spells for freedom and magical work for enhancing compassionate attitudes |

Depending on the exact time of the ritual, other celestial bodies will also have a strong effect on your magical work. In addition, you will need to take into consideration the seasonal energy of that time (see pages 134–139) and the phases of the Moon (see page 141).

ASTROLOGICAL CORRESPONDENCES

Wizards observed that there were a number of important links or correspondences between the energy of the Zodiac, the elements, herbs, stones, and metals. Here is a table that lists some of those relationships.

| Zodiac signs | Planets | Elements | Herbs | Stones, resins | Metals |
|---|---|---|---|---|---|
| Aries | Mars | Fire | Chili Pepper, Hemp | Ruby, Amethyst | Iron |
| Taurus | Venus | Earth | Cumin, Flax | Emerald, Moss Agate | Copper |
| Gemini | Mercury | Air | Meadowsweet, Vervain | Agate, Beryl | Quicksilver |
| Cancer | Moon | Water | Honeysuckle, Water Lily | Moonstone, Emerald | Silver |
| Leo | Sun | Fire | Saint John's Wort, Chamomile | Carnelian, Ruby | Gold |
| Virgo | Mercury | Earth | Lavender, Valerian | Aventurine, Jasper | Quicksilver |
| Libra | Venus | Air | Rose Geranium, Lemon Thyme | Turquoise, Diamond | Copper |
| Scorpio | Mars | Water | Basil, Wormwood | Sapphire, Topaz | Iron |
| Sagittarius | Jupiter | Fire | Dandelion, Agrimony | Amethyst, Garnet | Tin |
| Capricorn | Saturn | Earth | Comfrey, Henbane | Hematite | Lead |
| Aquarius | Uranus | Air | Star Anise, Myrrh, | Aquamarine, Sapphire | Aluminium |
| Pisces | Neptune | Water | Moss, Seaweed | Lapis Lazuli, Peridot | Lodestone |

# Tarot

The seventy-eight cards of the Tarot are a powerful form of divination, used from about the fourteenth century. Many a Wizard has also used the Tarot for spiritual guidance by meditating on a particular card for a particular purpose. The Tarot is divided into two parts — the Major Arcana and the Minor Arcana.

## THE MAJOR ARCANA

There are twenty-two cards in the Major Arcana. This group of cards refers to progress through life, and life's situations and challenges, and contains cards that represent the various types of people who may come into your life. Some Wizards believe each card has one meaning when pulled from the deck facing the right way up, but an opposite meaning if taken from the pack with the image upside down.

| Number and name of Major Arcana card | Positive meaning | Reverse meaning |
|---|---|---|
| 0 – The Fool | Starting a new venture | Experiencing a false start |
| 1 – The Magician | Gaining positive guidance | Failing to use the guidance well |
| 2 – The High Priestess | Gaining esoteric knowledge | Attracting hidden enemies |
| 3 – The Empress | Experiencing growth, fertility, increased creativity | Losing money and creative control |
| 4 – The Emperor | Needing to take responsibility and exercise discipline | Losing direction and showing weakness |
| 5 – The High Priest | Gaining spiritual wisdom | Rejecting restrictions |

| Number and name of Major Arcana card | Positive meaning | Reverse meaning |
|---|---|---|
| 6 – The Lovers | Experiencing choice and love | Finding infidelity or experiencing misunderstanding |
| 7 – The Chariot | Finding your direction in life | Feeling unfocused about your life's work |
| 8 – Justice | Needing to consider a decision carefully | Allowing impulse to affect a decision badly |
| 9 – The Hermit | Needing to withdraw to solve a problem | Refusing to take useful advice |
| 10 – The Wheel of Fortune | Allowing random or unknown factors to take their course | Experiencing delays outside of your control |
| 11 – Strength | Needing determination and persistence | Experiencing fear and indecision |
| 12 – The Hanged Man | Needing self-sacrifice before change can occur | Failing to learn the required lesson |
| 13 – Death | Experiencing transition and change | Experiencing frustration and dissatisfaction |
| 14 – Temperance | Needing harmony and time for healing | Experiencing difficulties in family and business relationships |
| 15 – The Devil | Experiencing the effects of pride and arrogance | Experiencing freedom and pleasure |
| 16 – The Tower | Experiencing major upheaval | Failing to see or tell the truth |
| 17 – The Star | Experiencing hope and optimism | Feeling stressed and unfulfilled |
| 18 – The Moon | Experiencing an absence of reason | Experiencing delays and hidden agendas |
| 19 – The Sun | Finding fulfillment | Feeling overexcited |
| 20 – Judgment | Experiencing a rebirth in ideas or development | Experiencing failure and inability to see the truth |
| 21 – The World | Finding ultimate success | Experiencing obstacles to success |

## THE MINOR ARCANA

The rest of the Tarot of fifty-six cards is further subdivided into four groups — the wands, cups, pentacles, and swords. Each group is representative of an element:

- The swords represent the element of Air, and symbolize human intelligence, the ability to pursue creative enterprises, and imagination.
- The cups represent the element of Water, and symbolize the ability to create and conduct relationships.
- The pentacles represent the element of Earth, and symbolize the ability to make money, acquire material possessions and create a home.
- The wands represent the element of Fire, and symbolize the ability to overcome obstacles and strengthen our will and purpose in life.

Each minor arcana suite has a King, Queen, Knight, and Page, followed by ten numbered cards.

The King usually represents a dominant male who is affecting your intellectual pursuits, if he is King of Swords (perhaps your teacher); your relationship, if he is King of Water (perhaps your lover); your monetary skills (perhaps your boss); or your purpose in life (perhaps your father). The King can also represent the acquisition of power.

The Queen represents an important woman supporting your ambitions. The Knight symbolizes an ambitious person or the idea that you will experience change soon, while the Page is a youngster who is affecting you, perhaps indicating that you will receive some news soon.

## HOW TO USE THE TAROT IN MAGIC

As each card of the Tarot has a particular psychic meaning (see the chart opposite), Wizards have used the Tarot to help them tap into current energy patterns. The Tarot can help predict the future and allow the Wizard to gain insight. However, it is a tool that points

to the potential of events and people if the patterns continue uninterrupted. If you do not like the way your path in life is leading, use the Tarot to help you see what you need to do to change your course. There are a number of patterns or spreads that you can learn to give you a full answer to your question.

The Tarot can be used in magic in many ways. You could focus on your specific question, shuffle the cards and clear your mind of any issue except the one to which you seek an answer. When you feel ready, pull a card from the pack and lay it on the table. It is important that you meditate on the image first before you look up the meaning (if you don't know it already).

You could also include the cards in your spell or other magical work, by deliberately choosing a card that represents the energy that you wish to invoke for your work. Look up the meanings on the previous pages and choose the most appropriate card. For instance, if you are doing a love spell, you may choose the Lovers card from the Major Arcana or the two of cups from the Minor Arcana. If you wish to ensure success for your spell, include The World card from the Major Arcana.

| Minor arcana numbered cards | Interpretations |
|---|---|
| Ace | Beginnings |
| 2 | Balance required |
| 3 | Growth |
| 4 | Stability |
| 5 | Uncertainty |
| 6 | Harmony |
| 7 | Endings |
| 8 | Balance achieved |
| 9 | Success |
| 10 | Completion |

# SPELLCRAFT

## THE POWER OF SPELLS AND THE ETHICS OF MANIPULATION

S pells work because of the Wizard's ability to tap into a powerful energy source and to channel that power and his own energy and will towards a particular purpose. Spells can be cast for all sorts of purposes and for all kinds of reasons. Magic in itself is neither evil nor good. It is the intention of the Wizard that colors magic for good or for evil.

This book outlines a large number of ways that magical energy can be used for benevolent, kind, and compassionate purposes — to help or protect people. Nevertheless, there are those Wizards who will dabble in magic in order to manipulate or harm another person or to consort with dangerous spirits.

There are innumerable grimoires that instruct on occult ways to cause damage. However, the price of such magic is very high and can include grave illnesses, mental disturbances, and extreme ill fortune.

If he conducts spells of harm, the Wizard will find that he will eventually be caught in an unpleasant cycle of using negative energy and having to maintain shields of protection constantly in order to avoid the rebound. The energy required for this kind of imprisonment in negativity is very high, and some unwise Wizards will be tempted to call on evil spirits to help keep these negative energies at bay. Unfortunately, these supernatural entities also extract a heavy price, a price that may even end the Wizard's life prematurely. Please treat magic with caution and only perform those spells and magical workings that produce positive results for yourself or your friends and clients.

## The Power of Invisibility

There are a number of different types of spells for achieving "invisibility." There is some doubt whether true invisibility can be achieved, although a number of grimoires have given complex, and sometimes gruesome, instructions on how to achieve true invisibility.

One such spell, from *The Grimorium Verum* (thought to have been published by "Alibeck, the Egyptian" in 1517), required a Wizard to have a strong stomach, as it involved burying a dead man's head with black beans stuffed in its eyes, ears, and mouth. The Wizard was then instructed to water the head with brandy of the best quality for a number of days until he conjured a spirit. However, various spirits often sought to trick a Wizard into believing that they were the right one, so a Wizard had to be prepared to question the spirit closely and have the appropriate passwords.

A very simple way of becoming if not invisible, then at least inconspicuous, is to visualize your body surrounded by a cocoon of blue light. As soon as you feel completely surrounded by the light, you will find that people are not able to focus on you, leaving you free to move about and away from any dangerous situation. However, this tends to work only if you do not make any sudden or dramatic movements. For an ancient Celtic spell to help you become inconspicuous, see page 46.

### Invisibility Stone

*Wrap a stone called Ophethalminus within a leaf of the bay tree and carry it within your hand to become invisible.*

## The Power to Fly

A sure sign of Witchcraft was the ability of a man or woman to fly on a broomstick, or simply to fly and be somewhere else in an instant. Strangely, although this would have been a useful skill to have during the Spanish Inquisition, this propensity was not noted by the examiners and torturers of those accused of Witchcraft in the sixteenth century.

Since time immemorial, the ability to be in two places at the one time (called bilocation magic) or to fly has fascinated Wizards and other occult practitioners. The ability to astral travel (the art of traveling spiritually while leaving the body to rest undisturbed in a safe place) has piqued the curiosity of Wizards for centuries. In ancient Egypt, a magician or priest was often trained in the ability to astral travel.

Astral travel works on the premise that we are all made up of several strata of different types of bodies. In ancient Egypt, it was believed that the body has seven layers, ranging from the physical body (called *khat*), through the spiritual (called *buddhi*) to the divine (called *atma*).

It can be speculated that some of the ointments and mixtures that reputedly gave a person the ability to fly had in fact very strong hallucinogenic properties. However, some of the unguents could also have had the psychic ability to allow the spirit to roam free, going to places far from the body but able to retain its senses.

Wizards needed to train so that their spirits could return with intact memories of what had been seen and heard.

Broomsticks, in the early Ages, were apparently a popular form of travel.

## The Power to Control the Weather

Ancient Druids (see pages 44–47) unnerved Christian missionaries by apparently conjuring a sudden storm or heavy fog.

Other methods of weather control were practiced by sailors. Fearing inclement weather on their journey or the lack of wind to bring them home, knots were tied in their handkerchiefs. In other cultures, shamans would conduct rituals to appease the spirits of the earth so they would grant rain in times of drought.

A number of ancient grimoires include detailed instruction on how to control the weather or create disruptions, such as earthquakes. The *Book of Spirits*, otherwise known as *Lemegeton*, informs us that a powerful, high-ranking genie called Procel was responsible for helping magicians to conjure the illusion of heavy rain and thunder.

Weather magic often involves strong concentration and powerful visualization skills. To whip up a strong wind, one spell requires a practitioner of magic to visualize the feeling of wind through his hair and to imagine that the wind is increasing in power. Chanting has also been known to bring about rain:

*Rain, rain, come today*
*Wait no more another day.*

### Wizard's Tip

*Sometimes a Wizard will be spared from wasting his energy
on creating a spell to bring about rain because already he will
have observed certain signs and omens that rain will soon come.
These omens include:*
- *swallows flying low over the land;*
- *spiders leaving their outdoor webs;*
- *soot falling down the chimney.*

## The Power of Numbers

Numbers continue to have a magical status in the occult world. The tradition dates back to the time of Pythagoras, a sixth-century BC Greek philosopher and mathematician, who connected the energy of numbers with certain aspects of the Cosmos and the material world.

Among others, Francis Barrett, in *The Magus* (1801), examined the symbolism of numbers, particularly two to twelve. He commented:

*The doctrines of mathematics are so necessary to and have such an affinity with magic, that they who profess it without them are quite out of the way, and labour in vain, and shall in no wise obtain their desired effect.*

**Two:** Barrett started with two as the "first multitude" and considered it a number of mutual love and charity, although Pythagoras believed "duality was a devil, and an evil intellect."

**Three:** This number is very special in religious ceremonies as it is a holy number and a symbol of perfection. Barrett points to how "all magnitude is contained in three," naming such famous threes as the three hierarchies of angelical spirits and the three powers of intellectual creatures — memory, mind, and will.

**Four:** This is another extremely important occult number. Pythagoras considered it the "foundation and root of all other numbers." It also relates to many naturally occurring phenomena, such as the four seasons and the four elements "under heaven."

**Five:** Five was believed to be symbolic of justice because it divides the number ten "in an even scale"; it is also thought to correspond to a human being, who, with arms and legs outstretched, forms the five points of a pentagram.

**Six:** Six was considered the day of man, because on the sixth day, humans were created. However, it was also considered to be an evil number, as 666 was the number ascribed to the "beast

*Even numbers represent stability, male energy and luck, while odd numbers symbolize creativity and female energy.*

of the apocalypse" (a sobriquet that was also gleefully adopted by Aleister Crowley — see pages 30–31).

**Seven:** Seven was believed to refer to the "mystery of time," with the seven celestial bodies being named after the seven days of the week. Seven also refers to the seven colors of the rainbow, and so can be used in spells seeking unity. It can also be considered as a number of regeneration, as it is believed that the body regenerates itself in seven years.

**Eight:** Eight is a number connected with material possessions. Barrett refers to the priest's eight ornaments — a breastplate, coat, girdle, mitre, robe, ephod (a richly embroidered apron worn with shoulder straps), girdle of the ephod, and golden plate.

**Nine:** Astrologers observed that major changes tended to occur in a person's life at the end of each cycle of nine years. Astrologers noted that at this time a person would often experience major changes. Nine is also useful in healing spells.

**Ten:** Ten is considered a "universal number, complete, signifying the full course of life."

**Eleven:** Eleven is an odd number that is stuck between the two completion numbers — ten and twelve. As a result, the number often signifies repentance and insignificance. The number could be used for "invisibility" spells.

**Twelve:** Twelve is the number of "grace and perfection," and has been considered a number of completion, and of the "chosen."

# THE KABBALAH

## THE STRUCTURE OF THE PHYSICAL AND PSYCHIC WORLDS

The Kabbalah (also spelt "Cabala" or "Qabala") is an ancient magical Hebrew system that orders the energies of the world and the universe by using the image of the Tree of Life. The Tree of Life consists of ten levels of energy flows, called the sephiroth.

To advance his spiritual development, the Wizard will conduct certain practices that allow him to understand the spiritual meaning of each level (or sephirah) and help him progress toward deeper insights about his psyche. The following ten levels, starting at the base of the Tree of Life, are:

Malkuth — Beginning of Creation: earthly preoccupations

Yesod — Foundation: sexual drives and creativity

Hod — Splendor: the intellect and reason

Netzach — Victory: love and the emotions

Tiphareth — Beauty and Harmony: the Messiah

Geburah — Severity and Strength: the warring God

Chesed — Mercy and Order: the compassionate God

Binah — Understanding: the Great Mother

Chokmah — Wisdom: the Great Father

Kether — Crown of Creation: infinite bliss

There are many ways of studying this complex and fascinating system of magic. Wizards have always cherished ways of tapping into the power of the Divine, and the Kabbalah was an excellent system of hierarchy leading the Wizard to higher understanding.

The Kabbalists also created combinations of numbers, formed in what came to be known as "magic squares", which resonated

with the seven celestial bodies — Sun, Moon, Mercury, Venus, Mars, Jupiter and Saturn. A complete list of magic squares for each celestial body is reproduced in the glossary on pages 144–147).

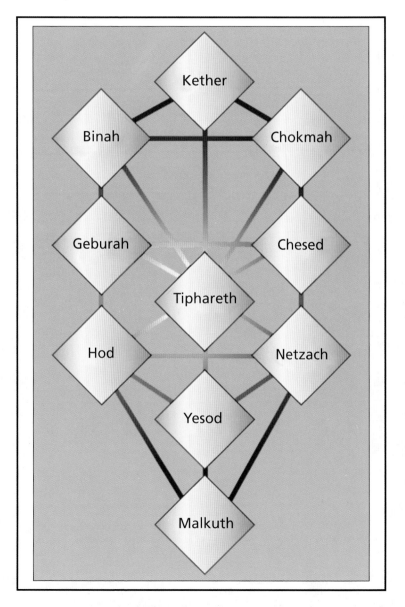

## Ceremonial Magic

In many magical traditions it is believed that magic should be performed according to certain procedures so that Wizards or Witches may work to create a profound change within their own lives or the life of others while being protected from any undesired influences hampering this work.

Secret sects and covens often devised rituals to teach new members or initiates the various secrets of magic and of existence. Each ritual that postulants undertook would lead them to deeper insights into themselves, their world, and the worlds beyond. Each ritual would also give the postulant an opportunity to put new learning to use.

Another aspect of Ceremonial Magic is that, like the ingredients of spells, the ritual is devised so that the highest possible number of correspondences is invoked. Correspondences refer to the belief, which is strongly practiced by the Kabbalists, that each element of the physical and psychic worlds has a certain vibration that has the power to enhance a particular magical purpose.

Each supernatural entity, and each planet, element, animal, tree, herb, flower, metal, mineral, stone, and any other living substance, has vibrations that are magically connected. For instance, to ensure that a ritual successfully attracts love, a Wizard would invoke the energy of the planet Venus.

In such a ritual, the Wizard would invoke the presence of the Goddess Venus, the spirits and intelligences of Venus, and the elements, particularly Water; if he were a Kabbalist, he would also include the magical numbers and divine names that correspond to the appropriate sephirah, in this case Netzach.

A number of grimoires gave the names of the particular devils who could be invoked and forced to do the Wizard's bidding. However, many a Wizard has met peril when performing such magic.

Grimoire image relating to the manufacture of a protective magical circle, for the conjuration of demons. From a seventeenth century English grimoire. Note the *Agla*, and the variant sigil for the Seal of Solomon.

Ceremonial Magic has the advantage of creating a safe place for a Wizard to work his magic undisturbed and without the interference of negative energies, in either human or spirit form. It is an excellent way of "working between the worlds," giving the Wizard the best opportunity to make the desired change.

In a ritual, one of the first actions is to purify the area used for the rite. There are many ways of doing this. One of the simplest is to sprinkle salt on the ground where the ritual will be performed. A circle is then cast around the Wizard and anyone else who has been invited to participate in the "working." Wizards often work within a circle, which is traditionally nine feet (3 m) in diameter, and is constructed by visualizing a light or fog swirling around the perimeter of the circle. Within this psychic circle, the Wizard is safe from harm and disturbance, and can focus fully on the magic at hand.

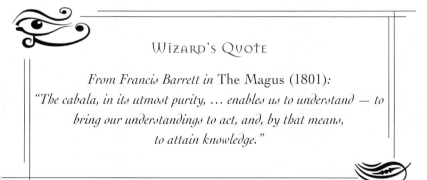

### Wizard's Quote

*From Francis Barrett in* The Magus (1801)*:*
*"The cabala, in its utmost purity, … enables us to understand — to bring our understandings to act, and, by that means, to attain knowledge."*

# WIZARDLY HELPERS

## ANGELS, SPIRITS AND GENIES

There are a number of systems that try to explain the hierarchy of supernatural entities such as angels and spirits. The Kabbalah's view of the structure of the physical and psychic worlds is believed to have derived from a system given to Adam by the angels after his eviction with Eve from the Garden of Eden, so that human beings would have a way of reconnecting with God.

Particular "intelligences," or presiding good angels, were believed to be part of the energy force of each celestial body. Francis Barrett, in *The Magus* (1801), gives the following corresponding presiding intelligences:

The Hebrew names of the intelligences are inscribed on

| *Celestial body* | *Corresponding intelligence* |
|:---:|:---:|
| Sun | Nachiel |
| Mercury | Tiriel |
| Venus | Hagiel |
| Mars | Graphiel |
| Jupiter | Johphiel |
| Saturn | Agiel |

talismans to invoke the energy of the particular celestial body for the appropriate magical purpose. However, Wizards have always been warned not to include the name of the spirits or demons of the celestial body on any talisman.

Spirits and genies are the subject of innumerable grimoires. Barrett's *The Magus* even contained color plates of the gruesome visages of some of the spirits, such as Astaroth and Mammon. The ability to control troublesome spirits was allegedly given to

King Solomon (see pages 10–11), who used a ring that had been engraved with a pentacle by the archangel Michael.

The grimoire *The Key of Solomon The King* focused on various methods of controlling spirits for the Wizard's particular purpose. These spirits had a propensity for trickery, and relied on the Wizard's ignorance so they could deceive and harm him.

One of the most famous grimoires on the topic was the *Lemegeton* or *Book of Spirits*. This book listed the various spirits or demons and itemized their rank in the supernatural world, including the seventy-two genies who were once captured in a brass vessel by King Solomon but were released unwittingly in later, still ancient, times. Many of these genies have both malevolent and benevolent traits, and they should all be treated with extreme caution.

The Wizard would be able to call upon them from within the safety of his magical circle (see pages 120–121). In his preparation the Wizard would have also enclosed his circle within a triangle. When called, the spirit or genie would only be able to occupy the space between the circle and the points of the triangle, the Wizard steadfastly refusing the spirit access into the circle and carrying two powerful forms of protection — the "Pentacle of Solomon" and the "Seal of Solomon."

The Pentacle of Solomon is a design derived from the five-pointed star, while the Seal of Solomon is a six-pointed star. The Wizard is instructed to make the Pentacle from virgin calfskin and the Seal from virgin parchment.

A series of pentacles, seven-jointed stars and heptagons were engraved on a plaque (The Seal of Aemeth) which was used by Dr John Dee (see pages 22–23) to conjure benevolent angels.

## Familiars and Power Animals

Animals and birds were believed to be psychically sensitive and were of great help to all the Wizards or Witches who focused their magic not so much on celestial observances as on reverence for nature. While some Wizards were known to invoke certain spirits or genies, like Duke Amduscias, to grant them a familiar, there are other, less troublesome ways of finding the right familiar.

Familiars are the consorts of Witches and Wizards. They were believed at one time to be low-ranking spirits, demons or imps, frequently taking the form of animals, with the ability to protect their master or mistress. They were reputedly able to carry out low-level forms of mayhem, such as the curses of their masters or mistresses. This idea of the familiar was prevalent during the "Burning Times," in the late fifteenth and early sixteenth centuries, when many were burned on charges of practicing Witchcraft and consorting with the Devil.

In modern-day magical practices the Wizard is very respectful of the energies of birds and animals, following a combination of Druidic and shamanistic practices, such as observing the movement of the birds and animals to deduce the energy flows and disturbances within the earth, weather changes and other phenomena that may affect the survival of a community.

## Wizard's Tip

*To attract a familiar, follow these six steps:*

*1. At the time of the New Moon, sit in a quiet place where you will not be disturbed and face either West or whichever direction you believe corresponds to the element of Water.*

*2. Clear your mind and imagine a shining ball of soft light in front of you.*

*3. Imagine that this light is the energy of your familiar, who will help you get in tune with your intuition and your psychic abilities.*

*4. Breathe in to the count of four, and breathe out to the count of four until you strongly feel the presence of this ball of light.*

*5. When ready, let the ball go and imagine that it has gone to get the right animal, bird, or reptile for you.*

*6. Go for a walk with the purpose of being shown your familiar. The first animal you see after you have completed steps 1 to 5 will be your familiar. It may be your family pet or a wild creature that will be with you, whether you see it or not, whenever you need to tap into your magical self.*

A shaman often calls for, or is "given," the gift of a power animal. This type of animal is a link between the shaman and the spirit world of teachers and ancestors in Native American traditions. This familiar helps the shaman get in touch with his intuition and understand the nature of a problem confronting his tribe.

A shaman may have a number of familiars or power animals, reptiles or birds to help him "see" as they would see. Hawks help the shaman see the big picture with clarity, while an owl imbues the shaman with wisdom and deep understanding. The wolf, bear, and other animals known to the shaman, may also come to him in a dream to help him with a particular problem.

## CHAPTER 5

# WHAT MUST A WIZARD KNOW?

## INTRODUCTION: UNDERSTANDING THE ENERGY FLOW OF THE COSMOS

Rituals and magical practices are fueled by the Wizard's will and his ability to tap into the power of the earth and the Cosmos. Wizards often find that when they are not properly tapped into the energy source of the earth, their magical workings leave them feeling drained and listless. When the Wizard is grounded into the earth, he is able to fuel his magical working by being a channel between the magical working and the self-renewing energy source of the earth, one that is the perfect combination of the four elements of Earth, Air, Fire, and Water.

However, the energy source of the earth is affected by the flux and mix of these elements. During each season, one element is generally predominant, being affected by the balance between day and night and the corresponding energies of the Sun and Moon.

| Element | Corresponding season |
|---------|----------------------|
| Earth   | Winter               |
| Air     | Spring               |
| Fire    | Summer               |
| Water   | Autumn               |

Over the centuries, a myth came to be told of the cycle of the seasons and the constant struggle between opposing energies (see pages 134–135). In nature, these opposing energies are seen in the balance between night and day, between the Moon and the Sun, between good and evil in certain mythologies, and in the duality between male and female energies in human beings.

A wise Wizard takes into account these seasonal energy fluxes and styles his magical workings for the appropriate season (see pages 136–139). Many Wizards have a deep reverence for nature and will also celebrate the eight seasonal festivals — there is one approximately every six weeks — that mark important shifts in seasonal energies.

The energy of the earth is not necessarily a constant flow. There are special places in the world that feel more powerful than others, and the Wizard should be aware of these areas so that he can either avoid their negative energies or can tap into those energies that are more attuned to magical workings. Places of magic can be found by referring to the flow of ley lines in a particular area (see pages 128–129), by developing the skills of dowsing (see pages 130–131) and using the pendulum (see pages 132–133).

### Wizard's Tip

**Getting Grounded**

*One of the simplest ways of becoming grounded after doing a magical working, such as a spell, is to take your crystal ball or pentacle or even a heavy rock, and push it into the ground, visualizing your energy flowing down into the earth to catch the flow of its energy. Visualize this energy moving up your arms and into your body. Feel it flow and circulate within you, making you feel strong and connected to the ground.*

# EARTH ENERGIES

## LEY LINES

The concept of a network or power grid of energy lines connecting centers of heightened charges of psychic energy was developed, or perhaps rediscovered, by Alfred Watkins in 1925. It is believed that these psychic energy centers were marked by natural formations such as mountain peaks, springs and pools, and artificially made additions to the landscape.

Places such as churches, monasteries, earthworks, and groups of standing stones, such as those at Stonehenge and Avebury, were powerful artificial centers. It is thought that ancient civilizations understood the power of the earth's energy fields and only built their sacred sites at ley centers.

Interestingly, many Pagan and Christian sites favored hills for the placement of their spiritual buildings and constructions — the Christian Church wished to be closer to its God, visualized as swelling above his creation. It is believed that the striking of blows to shape the stones that were part of a Pagan circle or a Catholic monastery helped to link the stones, which were usually imported from quarries from other sites, to their resting place at the points of ley line intersections.

Spellcraft and magical ritual were thought to have been more successful if the spell or ritual were performed at ley centers where spiritual worship was repeatedly conducted. It is believed that the psychic energy of a ley center is particularly powerful during the phase of the full Moon.

A network of lines is also thought to be an important tool in finding ley centers that have not yet been charted. A "ley hunter" will draw, on a map, lines from one known ley center to another.

Some of these lines concentrate in particular areas, such as Glastonbury, Saint Michael's Mount (the mount that stands off the Cornish coast in England), Stonehenge, and Avebury.

A ley center is usually an area through which at least seven ley lines intersect. However, even at places of a lesser number of intersections, also called "nodes," people have reported the experience of psychic phenomena, ranging from strange energy readings through to hauntings and levitation. Reports of sightings of unidentified flying objects also appear to occur at these intersections.

Glastonbury Tor, a major ley center, with straight ley lines connecting it with Stonehenge and Avebury, has been the subject of many legends. It is the supposed burial site of King Arthur and Guinevere, and is an area where fairies, extra-terrestrials, and even Merlin have been sighted. It is also believed to be the hiding place of the Holy Grail.

Wizards, druids, and other practitioners of magic were often consulted about the position of ley lines and ley centers. One of the instruments they used for finding leys was the sighting staff, which was used to draw the lines between two ley centers. The sighting staff was thought to be the precursor of the Wizard's magic wand.

St Michael's Mount at dawn on the coast of Cornwall, UK.

## Dowsing

Dowsing is the ancient art finding water, treasure, and even ley lines by sensing the small movements or sounds made by a two-pronged rod held in the dowser's hand. Sometimes called "water witches" or "water wizards," dowsers were often used by early farmers who needed help in deciding where to sink their new wells.

The traditional forked "rod" was made from a particular type of wood picked at an appointed time. Hazel that was picked at the time of the waxing moon was thought to be particularly successful for a dowsing rod for finding water. A number of traditions evolved about preparing the dowsing rod. For instance, it was believed that if the wood was obtained at Midsummer's Eve, the rod would be most effective at finding treasure.

Some modern dowsing rods are made from two steel rods that are bent at right angles. Often one end of the steel rod is pointed and the other end is encased in copper. The dowser holds one rod in the right hand and the other in the left hand. It is believed that the rods must be marked for the right or left hand and should never be switched around.

Before any dowsing can be done, the Wizard dowser must remove all jewelry, watches and glasses. Holding his head upright and his body as straight as possible, he must walk forward with the rod in front of him, visualizing the object of his search. Visualization skills must be strong in a dowser as he or she walks over the suspected territory. The dowser will feel a pulling or vibration emanating from the rod when he or she approaches the desired object. It is believed that the rod will pull particularly strongly if the object is very large.

Some dowsers have observed that, irrespective of their visualization of the object of their search, if they feel a pull on the left-hand side of the dowsing rod, they have most likely tapped

A dowser reading the secret language of the earth.

into the vibrations given off by an underwater stream or body of water. If they feel a pull on the right-hand side of the rod, they have tapped into the stream of energy that tends to be flowing along a ley line (see pages 128–129).

A famous dowser of the twentieth century, by the name of Thomas Lethbridge, explored the dowsing potential of the pendulum, which is a stone or metal tied to the end of a length of string, cotton or thin chain. Dowsers sometimes use pendulums, usually on a fairly short length of string, to find water and other energy flows. Lethbridge explored the use of different lengths of chain to hone the correspondence between the energy vibration and a particular type of object (see pages 132–133).

## Using a Pendulum

A pendulum, once used as a dowsing tool to find water, energy flows, and treasure underground, came to have a more sophisticated use in the twentieth century by picking up on subtler forms of vibrations. Thomas Lethbridge, a very successful dowser, began to experiment with a pendulum, finding that the pendulum reacted to different substances at different lengths.

The pendulum was not very useful to the dowser unless it was held on a short string and there was no wind around. Lethbridge found that differences in the lengths of the string, cotton, or chain attached to his pendulum (which was made from hazelwood) were an important factor in picking up vibrations from different types of substances. He deduced that when the length of string was 24 inches (60 cm), the pendulum picked up male energies. When his wife held it at 29 inches (73 cm), the

pendulum picked up female energies. Other correlations also occurred, such as 22 inches (55 cm) for silver and lead.

Lethbridge eventually found that the pendulum's use did not have to be confined to identifying the nature of an object or energy flow buried underground. It could also be used to give answers to questions on a number of topics, such as health and divination. The use of the pendulum for divination was not a new concept, but Lethbridge, through his experimentation, was able to extend the range of what the pendulum could do.

Most New Age stores have pendulums in stock, ranging from small metal weights through to semi-precious stones and artificial, faceted lead "crystals." The pendulum, when hanging freely from its string, is wide at the top and tapers down to a point at the bottom. There are many theories about what material the string should be made of to give the most accurate reading. Some believe that string from natural fibers is the most effective, while others prefer horsetail.

To experiment with a pendulum, hold the length of string in your right hand (or your left hand if you are left-handed) and stabilize your elbow by resting it on a stable surface, such as a table.

Get used to the feel of the weight of the pendulum and observe whether the pendulum is moving slightly , either backward and forward or in a circular formation. If it is not moving at all, give it a little push and observe the pattern of its movements.

When you are ready, ask the pendulum a question, the answer to which you know to be "yes." For instance — "Is my name [your real name]?" The pendulum will swing in a particular formation, clockwise, anticlockwise or to and fro. Repeat the experiment with a question to which the answer is "no." Practice with the pendulum to get a true sense of when it is giving you consistent indications of "yes" and "no." Hold the pendulum over a map or a floor plan and ask it to give you the location of something that you have lost. Experiment with the pendulum, and see if you can find some treasure!

# THE SEASONS

## THE CYCLE OF THE YEAR

There are eight seasonal festivals that are now celebrated by a broad range of magical practitioners who revere Nature and its energies. The festivals are approximately six weeks apart; four of them celebrate the summer and winter solstices and the spring and autumn equinoxes. These are called the lesser sabbats, and are markers of the change of the seasons.

The greater sabbats are four festivals that mark the height of the season's energy. Here is a table of the eight seasonal festivals, giving the dates for both the northern and southern hemispheres.

| Sabbats (Wiccan name) | Other names | Purpose | Northern hemisphere | Southern hemisphere |
|---|---|---|---|---|
| Samhain | Halloween | Height of autumn energy | 31 October | 1 May |
| Yule | Winter Solstice | Beginning of winter energy | 21-23 December | 21-23 June |
| Imbolc | Candlemas | Height of winter energy | 2 February | 1 August |
| Ostara | Spring Equinox | Beginning of spring energy | 21-23 March | 21-23 September |
| Beltane | May Day | Height of spring energy | 1 May | 31 October |
| Litha | Summer Solstice | Beginning of summer energy | 21-23 June | 21-23 December |
| Lammas | Lughnasadh | Height of summer energy | 1 August | 2 February |
| Mabon | Autumn Equinox | Beginning of autumn energy | 21-23 September | 21-23 March |

Over the years, a myth evolved called "The Wheel of the Year." It explained the ebb and flow of energy through the year, following the passage of the Sun through the Cosmos. Wizards understand that the movement of the celestial bodies has a profound effect on our lives. They take particular notice of the cyclic nature of seasonal energy, attuning their magic to practice only those forms of magic that correspond with the energy of the season (see pages 136–139). They take into account not only the energy flows of the season, but also the position of certain planets in the sky (see pages 142–143).

To illustrate the seasonal shifts of the year, the myth personifies the Sun (see page 140) as a young God who is born at midwinter. This is the bleakest time of the year, a time when the old Sun God, dying since the height of autumn's energy, is ready to descend into the underworld. However, it has been understood since ancient times that it is at this point that new hope is born, personified as a young God.

The youngster deity grows to an adolescent by the beginning of spring, and by the height of spring's energy the Sun God takes a lover, in the form of a young earth Goddess. She falls pregnant and starts to increase during the height of summer, the beginning of the seasonal autumnal harvests.

In the meantime, the young God has reached his maturity by the height of summer, and through the beginning of autumn feels his energy ebbing away as the earth gives up its energy in preparation for winter. During winter, while the Goddess is raising the young God, the old God becomes the Lord of Death, awaiting his rebirth.

## Winter

Winter solstice signifies the start of winter energy, which is a very useful time for quiet contemplation, and the study of obscure occult texts that a Wizard has not had the time to look through during the year. It is also the time to look back on the year that has passed since the last winter solstice and to start making concrete plans for what the Wizard wants to achieve in the next year.

During this season, the Wizard will sense that the energy has gone underground; there is far more emphasis on communication with the spirits, and familiars, and on finding out information from the supernatural world. It is also a time for the Wizard to improve his intuitive processes and to practice his divination and prophetic skills.

At this time, when little activity happens at the surface, the Wizard will feel that a lot of thoughts and ideas are germinating under the surface. These can be tapped into to gain insight into his spiritual development and the strengthening of his Wizardly skills.

By the height of the winter's energy, the Wizard will feel a stirring of new creativity and new thoughts, ideas, and strategies that he would like to try in his magical work. He may feel inspired to let go of bad habits and to purify his space and his soul during this time, in preparation for the enthusiastic instability of spring.

## Spring

At spring equinox, the beginning of spring energy will imbue the Wizard with a feeling of newfound strength. Evidence of creativity and fertility abound during this time, and the Wizard may wish to conduct spells for fertility, the creation of new businesses, and the healing of old wounds.

The Wizard may also be involved in seeing to the planting of herbs that he will be harvesting at the beginning of summer's energy (see page 138). He will also plant trees and other plants as a symbol of giving something back to the earth, balancing the energy that the earth is expending in sending up new shoots and new energy. The Wizard will give each plant a blessing individually, protecting it so that it can reach its full potential.

The Wizard may also conduct spells for the attraction of new love. Love spells performed at this time will generally be for meeting a range of eligible partners who may be potential long-term partners. Spells for love conducted during the summer months focus on finding a committed lover, as this is the time of a much more mature energy, while spring is a time for fun and non-commitment.

Spring is a time for testing out new ideas that have germinated during the winter months. It is a great time to experiment with new ways of working magic. However, the Wizard must not focus on long-term projects at this point, as the spring months are a time of unstable energy flows, when massive gains jostle with major losses.

## Summer

Summer's solstice marks the start of the change from the unstable energy of spring to a more stable and mature period of fulfillment. This is an excellent time to harvest any herbs for use in magical procedures, as it is believed that the healing capacity of the herb has now reached its potential.

It is at this time that a Wizard assesses whether he has fully utilized his energies through spring. Many spells cast in spring should be coming to fruition in summer.

The energy of summer is the most balanced of all seasonal energies. The energy between day (the Sun) and night (the Moon) is coming into balance. The energies of the Sun God reach their peak at the height of the summer. This is also the time of the first harvests.

As the summer experiences that reaping of the earth's bounty, so too will a wise Wizard find he is reaping rewards from his magical work. It is at this time that the Wizard will receive acknowledgment, fame and monetary assistance.

The spells that are best performed at this time of the year are those for attracting love, fertility, financial support, and other outward rewards. This is also the time to take stock of where the Wizard is in life. What did he want that he did not get? Is he on the way to achieving what he wants from life? This is the time to itemize goals and to remember that the things he is reaping were put in motion during the quieter winter months and early spring.

## Autumn

The autumn equinox marks the beginning of autumn energy. This is a time for celebration and preparation. A Wizard celebrates the major harvests and assures himself that there is enough energy in the form of food and other essentials to last him through the winter months.

Wizards will also conduct rituals to give thanks for the harvest and are sometimes requested to bless some of the remaining seeds, to ensure that they will germinate again in spring after surviving the winter.

Male energy is beginning to wane as the harvests take the energy out of the earth. The Wizard will begin to focus on helping people deal with the darker issues of life, such as death, grief, and loss. One of the thinnest "veils" between the earth and the spirit world is present at Halloween (the 1st of May in the southern hemisphere). This is the time when the Wizard will conduct ceremonies to ask advice of the spirits and to pay homage to those who passed over during the previous year.

Magic spells that are most effective in the autumn months are those that help protect us from our weaknesses. Protection spells are generally successful during this period of the year. Autumn is also a time for getting rid of destructive and unnecessary old habits and assessing what we don't need any more, in terms of our mind, body and soul.

# PLANETARY ENERGIES

## The Sun

The celebrations of the seasons are essentially the celebration of the perpetual cycle of the Sun (see pages 134–139). The Sun is particularly potent at summer solstice and is an important of celebration. This is the time when certain psychic energies of anything that relies on the Sun to survive — herbs and flowers, for example — are believed to reach their full magical potential.

The Sun is symbolic of male energy and is often the symbol adopted by dominant male deities and those Kings who claim the "divine" right to rule a group of people.

Magic using the energy of the Sun includes spells and rituals designed to bring about success (see pages 76–77), honor, courage and fortune, and spells to enhance perception and understanding of worldly matters. The color of gold, bright yellow, the day Sunday and gold itself were all used in magic to evoke the psychic power of the Sun. In *The Magus* (1801), Francis Barrett lists some potent Sun images that can be inscribed on certain stones to protect and enhance celestial energy. For instance:

- To render a person invincible, to bring a successful close to a particular project or to prevail against fevers and the plague, inscribe on a ruby the image of a crowned king sitting in a chair wearing saffron-colored clothes and with a globe at his feet, clutching a raven to his chest.

- To be fortunate, rich and beloved, inscribe on a carnelian the image of a crowned woman standing in a chariot drawn by four horses, holding a mirror in her right hand and a staff in the left hand, and sporting a flame on her head.

## The Moon

The energy of the Moon aids us in the intuitive and secret aspects of life. That is one reason the phases of the Moon are especially important to magical work. The celebration of the Moon's phases (new moon, waxing and full, waning and dark) is called in Witchcraft the esbat, with the most powerful time of psychic power being during the phase of the full moon.

Each phase of the Moon is believed to correspond with one of three faces of the Goddess — Maiden, Mother and Crone.

New moon is thought to have the energy of the Maiden. The type of magic that is practiced at this time includes spells to ensure the success of new projects and new love. It is also a time to cast spells to attract more money and necessary material possessions.

Full moon is the time when the Goddess has reached her maturity, and this is usually the best time for the Wizard to perform healing spells and to do magical work to heighten his intuition, perhaps through divination. This is also the best time to make powerful amulets and talismans.

The most powerful time to make a talisman is when the full Moon occurs on a day of the week that corresponds to the celestial body governing the talisman (see page 71).

The phase of the waning moon and dark moon corresponds to the Crone, the wise old woman who has immeasurable experience and knowledge. This time is best for magical rituals or spells where the Wizard wants to lessen a threat or the chance of being victimized.

## THE OTHER CELESTIAL BODIES

Earth is depicted at the centre of the cosmos, circled by the seven planets.
The globe is made up of four elements – Earth, Air, Fire and Water.

In older forms of magic, seven celestial bodies were used in magic as a basis for attracting or repelling certain energies. These energies include the Sun (see page 140) and the Moon (see page 141).

There are important rules for the other five celestial bodies in magical lore — Mercury, Venus, Mars, Jupiter, and Saturn — relating to the images that the Wizard should inscribe in order to tap into their particular powers. The images should be engraved or scratched onto the particular stone that corresponds to the energies of that particular celestial body. Once the image has been made, the stone must be carried about to attract the power of that celestial body to it.

### Mercury
• To attain knowledge, eloquence, and the ability to cure fevers, inscribe on pumice the image of a handsome, bearded young man with winged feet who holds a dart in his right hand, and has a rod with a serpent entwined in his left hand.

- To attract good will, a keen sense of wit and good memory, inscribe on mica the image of a man (sitting upon a chair) who has eagle feet, a crest on his head and a cockerel of fire held in his left hand.

## Venus

- To attract benevolence and good favor, inscribe on a piece of lapis lazuli the image of a woman with the head of a bird and the feet of an eagle, holding a dart in her hand.
- To attract beauty and pleasant behavior from a man, inscribe and color on a piece of turquoise the image of a young girl clothed in long, white robes, with her hair flowing around her head and holding flowers in her right hand and a comb in her left hand.

## Mars

- To gain the power of enchantment, inscribe on a diamond the image of a man armed, riding upon a lion and carrying an upright sword in his right hand and the head of a man in his left hand.
- To gain courage and good fortune, inscribe on a garnet the image of a crowned and armed soldier carrying a long lance in his right hand.

## Jupiter

- To attain longevity, inscribe and color on a clear white stone the image of a crowned man clothed in saffron-colored robes, riding an eagle or dragon, and carrying a dart in his right hand.
- To attain prosperity and freedom from your enemies, inscribe on a clear white stone the image of a crowned, naked man seated on a chair borne aloft by four winged boys.

## Saturn

- To prolong life, inscribe on a sapphire the image of a dressed old man sitting upon a high chair with his hands over his head, holding a fish and with his feet resting on some grapes.

# GLOSSARY OF SYMBOLS

✝ **Ankh:** an Egyptian hieroglyphic symbolizing immortality.
**Astrological symbols:** these were developed over the centuries
and were strongly influenced by the symbols found in Cornelius
Agrippa's book *De Occulta Philosophia* (1533).

| | *Modern* | *Agrippa* |
|---|---|---|
| *Aries* | ♈ | V |
| *Taurus* | ♉ | ♉ |
| *Gemini* | ♊ | ♊ |
| *Cancer* | ♋ | ⊶ |
| *Leo* | ♌ | ♌ |
| *Virgo* | ♍ | ♍ |
| *Libra* | ♎ | ♎ |
| *Scorpio* | ♏ | ♏ |
| *Sagittarius* | ♐ | ↑ |
| *Capricorn* | ♑ | ♑ |
| *Aquarius* | ♒ | ♒ |
| *Pisces* | ♓ | ♓ |

**Circle:** symbolizes spirit.

**Elemental signs:** the four elemental signs use the triangle as the basic form:

**Fire:** the upright triangle indicates the upward motion of the flames.

**Water:** the upturned triangle indicates the motion of rivers running deep into the earth.

**Air:** the upright triangle with a line through it indicates that Air is perceived to harmonize with Fire.

**Earth:** the upturned triangle with a line through it indicates that Earth is perceived to harmonize with Water.

**Eye:** symbolizes the spirit within and can be used as a protection against evil. Often inscribed on amulets and on the prow of boats. The Eye of Horus is a particularly popular Egyptian symbol of the all-seeing power of the higher being.

**Hexagram (six-pointed star):** the Star of David is a symbol of the Jewish faith. In occult terms, the symbol is also known as the Seal of Solomon, symbolizing the harmonious balance of the four symbols of the elements; it is thought to "unveil all of nature's powers." Under Hermetic principles, the six-pointed star symbolizes the concept of "As Above, So Below." The star was also used as a symbol of the Hermetic Order of the Golden Dawn.

**Magic squares:** there is a magic square for each of the seven celestial bodies — Sun, Moon, Mercury, Venus, Mars, Saturn, and Jupiter.

| Sun | | | | | |
|---|---|---|---|---|---|
| 6 | 32 | 3 | 34 | 35 | 1 |
| 7 | 11 | 27 | 28 | 8 | 30 |
| 19 | 14 | 16 | 15 | 23 | 24 |
| 18 | 20 | 22 | 21 | 17 | 13 |
| 25 | 29 | 10 | 9 | 26 | 12 |
| 36 | 5 | 33 | 4 | 2 | 31 |

## Moon

| | | | | | | | | |
|---|---|---|---|---|---|---|---|---|
| 37 | 78 | 29 | 70 | 21 | 62 | 13 | 54 | 5 |
| 6 | 38 | 79 | 30 | 71 | 22 | 63 | 14 | 46 |
| 47 | 7 | 39 | 80 | 31 | 72 | 23 | 55 | 15 |
| 16 | 48 | 8 | 40 | 81 | 32 | 64 | 24 | 56 |
| 57 | 17 | 49 | 9 | 41 | 73 | 33 | 65 | 25 |
| 26 | 58 | 18 | 50 | 1 | 42 | 74 | 34 | 66 |
| 67 | 27 | 59 | 10 | 51 | 2 | 43 | 75 | 35 |
| 36 | 68 | 19 | 60 | 11 | 52 | 3 | 44 | 76 |
| 77 | 28 | 69 | 20 | 61 | 12 | 53 | 4 | 45 |

## Mercury

| | | | | | | | |
|---|---|---|---|---|---|---|---|
| 8 | 58 | 59 | 5 | 4 | 62 | 63 | 1 |
| 49 | 15 | 14 | 52 | 53 | 11 | 10 | 56 |
| 41 | 23 | 22 | 44 | 45 | 19 | 18 | 48 |
| 32 | 34 | 35 | 29 | 28 | 38 | 39 | 25 |
| 40 | 26 | 27 | 37 | 36 | 30 | 31 | 33 |
| 17 | 47 | 46 | 20 | 21 | 43 | 42 | 24 |
| 9 | 55 | 54 | 12 | 13 | 51 | 50 | 16 |
| 64 | 2 | 3 | 61 | 60 | 6 | 7 | 57 |

## Venus

| | | | | | | |
|---|---|---|---|---|---|---|
| 22 | 47 | 16 | 41 | 10 | 35 | 4 |
| 5 | 23 | 43 | 17 | 42 | 11 | 29 |
| 30 | 6 | 24 | 49 | 18 | 36 | 12 |
| 13 | 31 | 7 | 25 | 43 | 19 | 37 |
| 38 | 14 | 32 | 1 | 26 | 44 | 20 |
| 21 | 39 | 8 | 33 | 2 | 27 | 45 |
| 46 | 15 | 40 | 9 | 34 | 3 | 28 |

## Mars

| | | | | |
|---|---|---|---|---|
| 11 | 24 | 7 | 20 | 3 |
| 4 | 12 | 25 | 8 | 16 |
| 17 | 5 | 13 | 21 | 9 |
| 10 | 18 | 1 | 14 | 22 |
| 23 | 6 | 19 | 2 | 15 |

## Saturn

| | | |
|---|---|---|
| 4 | 9 | 2 |
| 3 | 5 | 7 |
| 8 | 1 | 6 |

## Jupiter

| | | | |
|---|---|---|---|
| 4 | 14 | 15 | 1 |
| 9 | 7 | 6 | 12 |
| 5 | 11 | 10 | 8 |
| 16 | 2 | 3 | 13 |

**Pentacle (upright):** the five-pointed star that represents the four elements and the spirit, and is a popular symbol for Witchcraft.

**Pentacle (upside down):** frequently symbolizing Satanism.

### Planetary symbols:

| | |
|---|---|
| ☉ | Sun |
| ☽ | Moon |
| ⊕ | Earth |
| ☿ | Mercury |
| ♀ | Venus |
| ♂ | Mars |
| ♃ | Jupiter |
| ♄ | Saturn |
| ♅ | Uranus |
| ♆ | Neptune |
| ♇ | Pluto |

### Seasonal symbols:

| | |
|---|---|
| ♏ | Autumn |
| ♈ | Spring |
| ♋ | Summer |
| ♑ | Winter |

**Wheel of the Year:** the eight spokes within a circle symbolize the cyclic nature of each of the eight Pagan sabbats.

# GLOSSARY OF TERMS

**Alexandrian:** Wiccans initiated by Alex and Maxine Sanders or stemming from those who have been initiated by them.

**Amulet:** an object with magical properties of protection.

**Aradia: Wiccan** name for the Goddess, derived from Charles Leland's manuscript *Aradia: the Gospel of the Witches*.

**Astral projection:** a technique to move the consciousness to the astral plane while leaving the body safely behind.

**Athame:** a black-handled knife used for casting a circle around sacred space. Witches and Wizards usually have their own personal athame, and it is bad manners to touch such a knife without permission. It is also an important elemental tool, symbolizing air.

**Ayurveda:** a complete system of medicine over 3000 years old, developed in India.

**Beltane:** one of the four Greater Sabbats. Known as May Eve in the northern hemisphere.

**Boline:** a white-handled knife used for cutting ingredients for a magical purpose.

**Book of Shadows:** a personal journal compiled by a Witch or Wizard containing spells, rituals, and observations.

**Chalice:** or ornamental cup, one of the elemental tools symbolizing water.

**Charge:** to imbue an object with psychic power.

**Charm:** a magical word or words that can be used as a protection.

**Circle:** a sacred space, usually thought of as a sphere of energy created when it is cast.

**Coven:** a group of witches, traditionally ranging in number from three to thirteen, who meet regularly to perform and discuss magic.

**Craft, The:** a popular name for Witchcraft.

**Divination:** techniques used to divine the future or a person's path. Such techniques include **scrying**, **tarot cards** and reading tea leaves.

**Enochian:** a system of communicating with the angels developed by Edward Kelly and Dr John Dee in the early seventeenth century.

**Esbat:** a ritual or meeting conducted during full moon.

**Familiar:** a spirit assisting a Witch or Wizard in magical work; can take the form of a small animal, bird, or reptile.

**Gaia:** the Greek Goddess of earth.

**Gardnerians: Wiccans** initiated by Gerald Gardner and associated priestesses, or stemming from those initiated by Gardner.

**God/Goddess:** divine energy that can be seen as polarized into male and female energies.

**Golden Dawn:** an **occult** order founded in the late nineteenth century. Otherwise known as the Hermetic Order of the Golden Dawn.

**Grimoire:** a book that compiles a number of spells, techniques, and mysteries that have been used over a period of time.

**Grounding:** the practice of connecting the body's energy with that of the earth.

**High Priest:** the male leader in a group working a ritual.

**High Priestess:** the female leader in a group working a ritual.

**Imbolc:** one of the four Greater **Sabbats**. Known as Candlemas in the northern hemisphere.

**Invoke:** to summon a spirit or energy form into oneself.

**Kabbalah:** a Jewish mystical tradition that structures the levels of existence by using the symbol of the Tree of Life with ten levels of consciousness, each level higher up the tree representing a step closer to infinite.

**Lammas:** one of the four Greater **Sabbats**. Also known as Lughnasadh in the northern hemisphere.

**Litha:** summer solstice.

**Mabon:** autumn equinox.

**Necromancy:** summoning the spirits of the dead to do the summoner's bidding.

**Occult:** relating to magic, usually in terms of hidden knowledge.

**Ostara:** spring equinox.

**Pagan:** a general term used for people who are not Christian, Jewish or Muslim.

**Pentacle:** a five-pointed star made of metal or other material that is the symbol of the four elements and the spirit and can be worn as a protection. The pentacle is also an important elemental tool symbolizing Earth.

**Pentagram:** a five-pointed figure that is used as a blessing by Witches and Wizards. If it is upright, with the point uppermost, the pentacle is a symbol of **Wicca**. If it is upside down, with the point at the bottom, the pentacle is a symbol of Satanism.

**Power animal:** an animal or thought form of an animal with specific psychic attributes or protective qualities.

**Runes:** magical symbols first used in ancient Nordic and Germanic cultures. They are inscribed on talismans and amulets, and can be used for divination.

**Sabbat:** the eight seasonal festivals of a **Wiccan** year.

**Samhain:** one of the four Greater **Sabbats**. Also known as Halloween in the northern hemisphere.

**Scrying:** a form of divination using reflective surfaces, such as a crystal ball.

**Sephiroth:** the ten levels of energies that form the Tree of Life in the Kabbalah.

**Shapeshifting:** the ability to change one's form at will.

**Sigil:** a special sign, which incorporates a form of magical energy.

**Skyclad:** naked. The term is derived from the translation of an Indian term meaning "clad by the sky" that was first used in reference to the practice of Witchcraft by Gerald Gardner.

**Talisman:** an object charged with a specific magical purpose.

**Tarot cards:** a deck of cards representing certain aspects of life, used for divination.

**Triple Goddess:** refers to the three faces of the Goddess: the Maid (virgin), the Mother, and the Crone.

**Visualization:** a technique for imagining certain images, used for getting in touch with the spiritual realities.

**Wand:** an important elemental tool symbolizing fire.

**Wicca:** Old English name for the practice of Witchcraft.

**Wiccan:** an individual, male or female, who practices a modern form of Witchcraft.

**Witch:** traditionally a female Witch. However, in modern times the term refers to both male and female Witches.

**Wizard:** traditionally a male magician or a male counterpart of a female Witch. However, in modern times a male Witch also carries the title of Witch.

**Working:** a magical ritual.

**Yule:** winter solstice.

# READING LIST

**M. & A. Adams**, *The Learned Arts of Witches & Wizards: History and traditions of white magic* (Sydney, Lansdowne Publishing Pty Ltd, 1998)

**M. Adler**, *Drawing Down the Moon* (Boston, Beacon Press, 1981)

**D. Ashcroft-Nowicki**, *Daughters of Eve: The Magical Mysteries of Womanhood* (London, Aquarian, 1993)

**F. Barrett**, *The Magus: A Complete System of Occult Philosophy* (originally in London in 1801)(York Beach, Samuel Weiser, Inc, 2000)

**A. Beattie**,

*The Girls' Handbook of Spells* (Sydney, Lansdowne Publishing Pty Ltd, 2000)

*Love Magic* (Sydney, Lansdowne Publishing Pty Ltd, 1999)

*Money Magic* (Sydney, Lansdowne Publishing Pty Ltd, 2000)

*Seasonal Living* (Sydney, Lansdowne Publishing Pty Ltd, 1999)

**A. Beattie & A. Wolf**, *The Girls' Guide to Spells* (Sydney, Lansdowne Publishing Pty Ltd, 2001)

**R. Buckland**, *Buckland's Complete Book of Witchcraft* (St Paul, Llewellyn Publications, 1987)

**P. Beyerl**, *The Master Book of Herbalism* (Washington, Phoenix Publishing Co, 1984)

**A. Crowley**, *777 Revised* (New York, Weiser, 1970)

**V. Crowley**, *Wicca: The Old Religion in the New Age* (London, Aquarian Press, 1989)

**S. Cunningham**,

*Wicca: A Guide for the Solitary Practitioner* (St Paul, Llewellyn Publications, 1988)

*The Complete Book of Incense, Oils and Brews* (St Paul, Llewellyn Publications, 1990)

*Cunningham's Encyclopedia of Magical Herbs* (St Paul, Llewellyn Publications, 1990)

*Earth, Air, Fire and Water* (St Paul, Llewellyn Publications, 1992)

*Magical Herbalism* (St Paul, Llewellyn Publications, 1989)

*The Magic in Food: Legends, Lore & Spellwork* (St Paul, Llewellyn Publications, 1991)

**N. Drury**, *The Occult Experience* (London, Robert Hale, 1987)

**D. Fortune,** The Mystical Qabalah (New York, Ibis Books, 1981 reprint)

**D. Fortune**, novels

*The Demon Lover* (London, Wyndham Publications, 1976 reprint)

*The Goat-Foot God* (London, Wyndham Publications, 1976 reprint)

*Moon Magic* (London, Wyndham Publications, 1976 reprint)

*The Sea Priestess* (London, Wyndham Publications, 1976 reprint)

*The Winged Bull* (London, Wyndham Publications, 1976 reprint)

**G. B. Gardner**, *Meaning of Witchcraft* (New York, Magickal Childe, Inc, 1982 reprint)

**J. & S. Farrar,**

*Eight Sabbats for Witches and Rites for Birth, Marriage and Death* (London, Robert Hale, 1981)

*The Life and Times of a Modern Witch* (London, Judy Piatkus (Publishers) Limited, 1987)

*Spells and How They Work* (London, Robert Hale, 1990)

*What Witches Do: The Modern Coven Revealed* (Washington, Phoenix Publishing Co, 1983)

*The Witches' God: Lord of the Dance* (London, Robert Hale, 1989)

*The Witches' Goddess: The Feminine Principle of Divinity* (London, Robert Hale, 1987)

*The Witches' Way: Principles, Rituals and Beliefs of Modern Witchcraft* (London, Robert Hale,1984)

**S. Farrar**, novels

*The Twelve Maidens: A Novel of Witchcraft* (London, Arrow Books, 1976)

*The Sword of Orley* (London, Arrow Books, 1978)

*Omega* (New York, Times Books, 1980)

**R. Guiley**, *The Encyclopedia of Witches and Witchcraft* (New York, Facts on File, 1989)

**R. Hutton**, *The Triumph of the Moon: A History of Modern Pagan Witchcraft* (Oxford, Oxford University Press, 1999)

**M. Jordan**, *Witches: An Encyclopedia of Paganism and Magic* (London, Kyle Cathie, 1996)

**E. Lévi**, *The History of Magic* (originally published in London, 1913) (York Beach, Samuel Weiser, Inc, 1999)

**M. Medici**, *Good Magic* (London, Macmillan, 1988)

**T. Moorey**,

   *Paganism: a beginner's guide* (London, Hodder & Stoughton, 1996)

   *Witchcraft: a beginner's guide* (London, Hodder & Stoughton, 1996)

**D. & J. Parker**, *The Power of Magic: Secrets and Mysteries Ancient and Modern* (London, Mitchell Beazley, 1992)

**I. Shah**, *The Secret Lore of Magic* (London, Rider, 1990)

**L. Spence**, *The Magic Arts in Celtic Britain* (originally in London and New York, 1945)(New York, Dover Publications, Inc, 1999)

**"Starhawk"**, *The Spiral Dance: A Rebirth of the Ancient Religion of the Great Goddess* (San Francisco, Harper & Row, 1979)

**D. Stein**, *The Women's Book of Healing* (St Paul, Llewellyn, 1989)

**D. Valiente**,

   *An ABC of Witchcraft Past and Present* (London, Robert Hale, 1984 reprint)

   *Natural Magic* (London, Robert Hale, 1985 reprint)

   *Witchcraft for Tomorrow* (London, Robert Hale, 1978)

**L. Warren-Clarke**, *The Way of the Goddess: A Manual for Wiccan Initiation* (Dorset, Prism Unity, 1987)

**A. Watkins**, *The Old Straight Track* (London, Abacus, 1977)

**C. Wilson**, *Aleister Crowley: The Nature of the Beast* (London, The Aquarian Press, 1987)

# PICTURE CREDITS

The publishers would like to thank the following for the provision of the pictures used in this publication. Full effort has been made to locate all the copyright owners of the images and we apologize for any omissions or errors.

**Charles Walker Photographic Collection**
cover: from *A System of Magic; or , a History of the Black Art*, 1727; page 16: mezzotint by Von Kreling to a 19th century edition of Goethe's *Faust*; page 19: portrait from the title page of *De Occulta Philosophia*, 1532; page 21: engraved portrait of Paracelsus; page 23: title page from the *Monas Hieroglyphica*, 1564; page 25: from Robert Fludd's *Utriusque Cosmi Maioris*, 1621; page 27: print after the original copperplate of 1783 by N. Thomas; page 33; page 43: detail from the Hunefer papyrus, from the Wallis Budge edition of *The Book of the Dead*; page 57: vignette from Joachim Frizius, *Summum Bonum*, 1629; page 60: from Michael Maier, Atalanta Fugiens, 1618; page 97: from J. D. Mylius, *Anatomia Auri*, 1628; page 121: from a 17th century English grimoire; page 131

**Cinetel Productions/Collection of Nevill Drury**
page 38

**Mary Evans Picture Library**
page 13: Eleanor Fortescue Brickdale illustration to Tennyson's 'The Idylls of the King'; page 15: J Segrelle in Allers Familj-Jurnal [Swedish] 6 December 1927; page 31: Harry Price Collection; page 49; page 142: Andreas Cellarius, 'Harmonia Macrocosmica'

**Oberon Zell-Ravenheart**
page 36: © 1984

**Photolibrary.com**
page 105: stained glass window depicting signs of the Zodiac; page 114: woodcut of witches and black cats broomsticks; page 129: St Michael's Mount, UK/Nigel Hicks

# ÍNDEX

# MetroBooks

An Imprint of Friedman/Fairfax Publishers

This edition published by MetroBooks by arrangement with Lansdowne Publishing

ISBN 1-5866-3756-8
1 3 5 7 9 10 8 6 4 2

For bulk purchases and special sales, please contact:
Friedman/Fairfax Publishers
Attention: Sales Department
230 Fifth Avenue, Suite 700
New York, NY 10001
212/685-6610 FAX 212/685-3916

Visit our website:
www.metrobooks.com

Commissoined by Deborah Nixon
Production Manager: Sally Stokes
Illustrations: Penny Lovelock and Sue Ninham
Designer: Stephanie Doyle
Editor: Avril Janks
Picture research: Joanne Holliman
Project Co-ordinator: Kate Merrifield

Set in Cochin & Mason on QuarkXpress
Printed in Hong Kong by South China Printing